QUIT PORN AND GET RICH:
THE UNSPOKEN RULE OF SUCCESSFUL PEOPLE

Martin Prescott

Copyright © 2018 Martin Prescott

All rights reserved.

No part of this publication may be copied, transmitted, or broadcast in any form in mass media without the author's express consent. The information in this book is not a substitute for professional medical advice, and it is not intended for medical diagnosis or treatment. In case of health problems and before starting/ending treatment, consult a specialist. Neither the author nor the publisher take any responsibility for any effects resulting from following the content and advice contained in this book, nor for the general mood that readers may experience after reading this publication. The author supports his thesis by referring to research and opinions which have been cited for educational purposes only. Each publication referenced should be read in its entirety and interpreted separately, outside the context of this publication. The author's opinions cannot be treated as scientifically supported claims. The author does not guarantee the reader wealth or improvement in his/her life in any sense of the word. The events of the main character's life have been adapted to fit the story. The names of the characters have been changed, and any resemblance to real life persons or situations is accidental.

ISBN: 978-1-7312-4701-8

CONTENTS

Dedication 5

Foreword 7

1. Introduction 9
2. System basics 19
   2.1. THE MOST COMMON PROBLEMS 19
   2.2. HOW IT WORKS 23
   2.3. SUPERNORMAL STIMULI 29
   2.4. CHEMICALS AND HORMONES 31
   2.5. WHERE DO WE BEGIN 38
3. What has been seen cannot be unseen 43
   3.1. REMEMBERING 43
   3.2. RESEARCH ON BRAIN PERFORMANCE 45
   3.3. PHYSICAL CHANGES IN THE BRAIN 48
   3.4. THE BRAIN IN ACTION 50
4. What is on our minds? 55
   4.1. PRECIOUS NOVELTY 55
   4.2. IDEAS PRODUCE VALUE 59
   4.3. MONEY DOESN'T GROW ON TREES (FIRST UNSUCCESSFUL BUSINESSES) 61
   4.4. MORE INFORMATION MEANS MORE OPPORTUNITIES. 66
   4.5. THE FIRST SUCCESSFUL BUSINESS 71
5. I'm the captain now 75
   5.1. INTANGIBLE ASSETS 75
   5.2. RESEARCH ON SELF-CONTROL 80
   5.3. DEVELOPMENT OF SELF-CONTROL 83
   5.4. WEAKNESS AS AN ADVANTAGE 88
   5.5. QUITTING PORN 92

6. Fight for your right… or negotiate 101
6.1. THE IMPORTANCE OF ATTITUDE 101
6.2. SELF-CONTROL IN NEGOTIATIONS 105
6.3. THE FUTURE IS NEGOTIABLE 114

7. Getting accustomed to risk 125
7.1. THE BRIGHT SIDE OF UNCERTAINTY 125
7.2. RESEARCH ON RISK-TAKING 128
7.3. A STEP INTO THE UNKNOWN 134

8. Patience is a virtue 143
8.1. NOTHING HAPPENS BY CHANCE 143
8.2. RESEARCH ON PATIENCE 147
8.3. THE FRUITS OF MY LABOR 150

9. Real people 159
9.1. BUILDING RELATIONSHIPS 159
9.2. JUMPING IN AT THE DEEP END 164

10. Experience of society 171
10.1. OLDER TEACHINGS 171
10.2. SPORT 180
10.3. THE PORNOGRAPHY INDUSTRY 181

11. Do your best 185

Afterword 191

Resources 193

DEDICATION

I dedicate this book in memory of all the great ideas and opportunities wasted as a result of watching porn.

FOREWORD

We all want to get rich. Every day, we pass jaw-dropping, luxurious cars in the street. We keep up with the latest technological innovations and we desire every new gadget that appears on the market. We imagine traveling to the four corners of the earth. We watch professional athletes and we want the same lifestyle they enjoy. We admire the mighty of this world and wonder what secret they know that allowed them to get where they are.

Then we each return to our homes and ritually devote ourselves to watching porn on the Internet, forgetting about our dreams. Visiting porn sites and masturbating after school—or in the morning, when classes start a little later—become routine for us. In the very beginning, with fresh excitement, we shared the best links and commented on newly discovered actresses. Later, it became as interesting as brushing your teeth: it became a daily habit which went on for years.

None of us even suspected that we had a chance to make our dreams come true and to someday get where we once wished so badly to be. That vision had become so distant that we didn't even think about making an effort to realize it. I wonder how our lives would have turned out if we had known that the enthusiasm for fulfilling our dreams would be eroded with every porno movie we watched.

1. INTRODUCTION

Life is short, don't waste it watching someone else's.

I am almost thirty years old. I am an investment banker (mergers and acquisitions) and a businessman. Every day, I deal with transactions for millions of dollars and I meet with serious entrepreneurs and investors. My responsibilities include selecting opportunities on the capital market, persuading very influential people to take advantage of these opportunities, and then collecting commission from the transactions. After hours, I invest in capital markets, develop my own start-up and help people execute their ideas. I often take on very large responsibilities and major risks. Most importantly, I love new ventures, traveling, and—above all—I love life, people, and myself.

However, a few years ago, before I discovered certain mechanisms and rules governing my body, I doubted that I would ever be happy and satisfied with my life. I was a lonely, shy grouch who didn't see the point of living. Under the mask of a happy-go-lucky guy and a hedonist, there was a lost little boy, constantly plagued by insecurities about his appearance, background, and material status. I did not have a job, any useful knowledge, or prospects. I squandered most of my time on simple entertainment, including pornography. In fact, pornography became the only pleasure I could find in life. When I turned off the videos with naked ladies, the world would become gray again. At some point, I wanted something more than just naked women on my computer screen and failure in almost every aspect of my life. I started to look for the causes of my defeat and I finally realized how grave my weaknesses were. Because I was able to name them and to overcome them, I gained the energy and the ability to deal with many of life's problems.

Many situations we face require a particular predisposition and specific behavior. We often can't behave properly, not only because of a lack of awareness, but also because of hindrances posed by our bodies. It is very interesting how much depends on the well-being and physical fitness of your body. Unfortunately, many people don't know much about the processes that drive it. I will do my best to make sure that thanks to this book you will learn about important issues related to your physical well-being and how to use them in practice.

Each human body is slightly different and feels differently, more or less intensely. The sensitivity to stimuli, active hormones, or psychoactive substances varies, but general laws and dependencies are shared and usually occur to the same degree. Nature created the healthily and properly functioning body of a man in a similar way. The human body strives to survive, procreate, and protect itself and its loved ones. These are the basic human needs that Abraham Maslow clearly defined in his pyramid of needs. However, eroticization, pornography, and masturbation can significantly disrupt this hierarchy or slow down the progression to higher levels, i.e., to a feeling of belonging, respect, fulfillment and realizing one's potential.

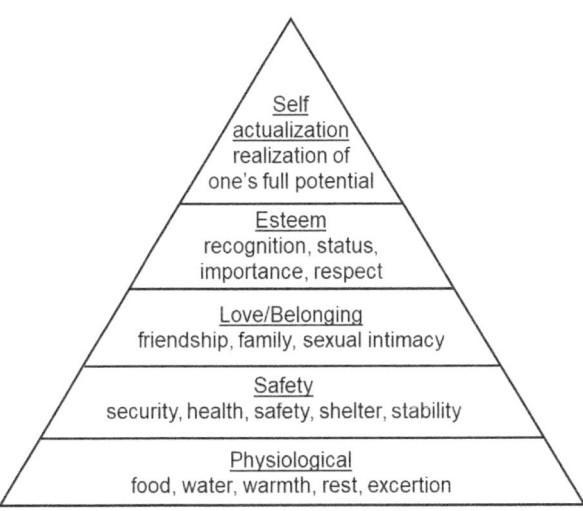

Naturally, success will not equate to achieving wealth for everyone. It can also mean living a happy, satisfying life, starting a family, or making achievements in a scientific, athletic, or professional career. Succumbing to sexual stimuli too often can lead us away from all these things. I describe the traits necessary to achieve success, which may be impaired by a habit of using pornography. In general, what I have in mind is how the drive for success works in effective and influential people and how it can be inadvertently reduced.

We have different predispositions, ambitions, and goals. Striving for perfection and achieving above-average results is not an obligation. We do not have to prove to ourselves and others what we are capable of. But what if we do not really know what we are capable of? What if we have not trusted our own skills so far? What if our natural abilities can allow us to attain much more, but we subconsciously suppress them? What if supernormal stimuli lead to helplessness, distraction, bitterness, laziness, and a lack of motivation? What if an excess of sexual stimulation causes a lack of self-confidence, fear, shyness, and a weak will? What if all this is hindering you from achieving success? Don't get me wrong, I don't believe that turning off porn is a recipe for success. I know people who have never watched porn but are unhappy with how their lives are going. However, you can be sure that excessive eroticization only seems like a trivial obstacle on the way to a happy life. Your life can be rich in experience, rich in professional successes, rich in kindness to others, rich in family happiness, and materially rich as well. Or you can spend it in front of the computer, watching strangers copulating.

I encourage you to forgive yourself because your willpower is likely too weak to deal with such strong tension. This book is not meant to intensify the guilt that may arise after masturbation. Reading it will help you to better understand the big picture, and to get to know yourself and your body better. I also encourage you to explore the issues raised here on your own after reading the book and to enlighten others. I want people to be aware of what excessive sexual stimulation does to the male body and what an impediment it is to achieving fulfillment in life. Unfortunately, these days, the pornography industry can imitate sexual relations more and more realistically and make a more and more addictive product with higher-quality movies, point-of-view (POV) camerawork, and virtual reality. For people using pornography, it is becoming increasingly difficult to resist these strong stimuli. You may be thinking that I'm exaggerating and that pornography isn't a problem, that it is just as normal as sex with a partner. I will explain why I have a different opinion on this subject and how much may depend on the inclination towards artificial sexual stimuli.

I discuss the problem of pornography mainly from the perspective of a heterosexual man, but all of the knowledge presented in this book is addressed to everyone, including women, who—according to statistics—are a growing group of Internet porn enthusiasts. It's worth raising awareness of this problem, regardless of gender, age, or sexual orientation. The book particularly applies to men going through puberty, entering adulthood, starting a career, settling down, and especially for those who aspire to success and contentment in life. The book was conceived in the name of social responsibility for the damage and alternative costs[1] which may come about and result from a tendency towards visiting pornographic sites. I feel obliged to prevent the unpleasant consequences of this problem and to give others the chance to make use of this knowledge as I did.

This is not yet another motivational book, which the shelves are lined with, providing nothing but a temporary boost to your mood. This book describes the real impact of eroticism, pornography, and masturbation on your performance in everyday life. It also explains how overcoming these propensities can vastly increase the chances of success in many areas. Your life without unnecessary eroticization can be active and focused. Do you know how successful people approach this problem? How pornography can prevent them from achieving their goals? How they find motivation and whether pornography can destroy it?

You won't find self-righteous moralizing in this book, I assure you. When I was a teenager, many people guilt-tripped me into avoiding sexuality and relations with the opposite sex. It did more harm than good. Conservative views on life seemed detached from reality, and sexual stimuli seemed less and less intimate and ubiquitous. I did not get the chance to learn credible arguments that would have dissuaded me from watching pornography. The conservative approach toward pornography turned out to be accurate, but this is only being proven today. When I was

---

[1] Alternative costs in this case refer to everything you could have accomplished instead of watching pornography.

young, no one told me that an excess of sexual stimuli could lead to such consequences as physical changes in the brain, sexual dysfunction, depression, chronic laziness, social anxiety, and—in extreme cases—disorders of the reproductive system. These are ailments which are easily diagnosed and which people should be particularly warned against. I want to draw your attention, however, to an area which is much more difficult to pinpoint, one which determines your success in life.

Reading this book will help you to comprehend the problem and to deal with it. Furthermore, it will help you to transform the tendency towards unnatural sexual stimuli into action and to achieve ambitious goals. While writing it, my intention was to help you, just as I once helped myself. I assure you that I have depicted everything with appropriate care and I haven't idealized anything. I am just an ordinary person who, until recently, hadn't realized the seriousness of this problem. You will recognize this in the everyday situations I describe, some of which will certainly seem familiar to you. Thanks to these experiences and to the discovery of the knowledge I wish to share with you, I have become a stable person and I am active in many areas. Since the publication of this book, I have also been subjected to pressure from the groups against whose interests it is addressed. Regrettably, while the porn industry earns so little from each of us[2], we have so much to lose—our lives.

In general, facts about the problem of pornography and guidelines on how to overcome an addiction to it are widely discussed and available on the Internet for free. I urge you to search for them. I discuss the problem of pornography in relation to business first of all and I extend the subject to

---

[2] The porn industry is worth billions of dollars because there are about a billion consumers. They make only a few dollars per user on average, but they charge fees for premium sites, sell personal data to their advertisers and third parties, or they earn on pay-per-click model.

many aspects which are vital to business and investing. I believe that the information presented here will aid you in being successful in life and in getting rich.

I had wondered for a long time what type of book this should be. I decided that the best and most objective approach would be to first refer the problem of pornography to everyday life and business, then to describe each issue from a scientific point of view (illustrating them with appropriate research), and finally to recount my own story, which paved the way to discovering this knowledge.

In my youth, I was always inquisitive—maybe even overly inquisitive. It was very rare for me not to look for answers to the questions that were bothering me. In time, I learned to access information on my own. This was also true in the case of health problems. In this book, I describe the harms and illnesses that may accompany watching pornography and masturbating too often. The majority of them will resolve after some time spent without these stimuli. If you suspect you're suffering from a more serious condition, consult a specialist. Don't be afraid to tell him or her about your habits. I sometimes suspected that I had various illnesses and I looked for answers by myself, which led to incorrect diagnoses and dejection over my supposed bad health. I even came close to treating diseases that I didn't have. I suspected bladder and prostate problems, and even cancer, among other things. All of these suspicions proved to be unjustified, something I learned only after doing expensive tests. Information about every potential disease is almost infinitely accessible, which is disastrous for the layman.

However, things were different when it came to pornography. Most of the popular sources available at the time simply trivialized the problem, turned it into a joke, or even regarded masturbation as good for one's health. I found such information in textbooks for adolescent boys, sex education classes at school, and "progressive" doctors. Unfortunately, the young mind quickly concludes from such information that pornography is harmless. I do share the opinion that occasional masturbation without watching pornography is not a problem. However, regular practice combined with pornography can lead to addiction and serious physical and psychological consequences which affect one's development and future life. Let me be more specific: occasionally means less than once a month, irregularly, while often means more than once a month, regularly.[3] It should be clearly stated that masturbation alone, without watching pornography, results only in a temporary fatigue of the body, which requires a bit of energy to rebuild the semen supply. Releasing the sexual tension built up by a natural libido will not result in physical or psychological problems. What changes masturbation into something unhealthy, against human nature (substantially increasing frequency and compulsiveness[4]), is pornography. You have undoubtedly noticed that masturbation without pornography takes much longer than with pornography and that it's only possible after some period of abstinence. This is because the mind of a man needs a sexual stimulus, which is a woman. The male body is not naturally able to conjugate with dozens of women within a few hours and to fertilize all of them. Pornography helps to fool the male brain, thanks to which masturbation can be easy, fast, and even very frequent. Unfortunately, this comes at a cost. Why is it that sporadic cases of such behavior may lead to increased frequency or addiction? Because pornography and masturbation provide massive, momentary pleasure, and in modern times they

---

[3] Of course, it depends on the individual. I've chosen these intervals to better illustrate the relevant norms.

[4] Compulsion in psychology is defined as "a strong, usually irresistible impulse to perform an act, especially one that is irrational or contrary to one's will";
http://www.dictionary.com/browse/compulsion

also provide an escape from everyday problems—just like hard drugs, where the mechanism of addiction is very similar.

As this book is being written (2017), statistics show that at least 2/3 of American men aged 18–49 regularly watch pornography. The vast majority of them are addicted and do not realize the position they are in. Some, however, suppose that such involuntary habits are not healthy for them. These doubts will not be confirmed by the aggressive industry based on human sexuality. People working in this industry will claim that watching pornography is a normal practice because they make a tremendous amount of money from it. What's more, they will push the falsehood that frequent ejaculations are healthy. Unfortunately, masturbating too often—upsetting the natural rhythm of the body—can have undesirable consequences. Also, remember that limiting sexual activity is not harmful to the body. The body will adapt[5] and use the previously unduly lost energy, micronutrients, and vitamins in a different way. At least 25% of pornography viewers are aware of the problem and are searching for a solution, but only a small percentage of them are able to break the habit on their own. Perhaps they are not yet aware of the benefits of this decision. This group experiences more and more frequent pangs of conscience that may lead to depression. There are also those who have learned about the pernicious effects of pornography, and have decided to give it up once and for all. I am one of those people.

When I started to enter adulthood, I realized that I don't want to just live my life, but I want to enjoy it, to achieve professional and personal success. When I started to suspect that watching pornography was adversely affecting my body, I started doing research. Thanks to that, I learned the complexity of the problem and understood the intricate

---

[5] Initially after pornography use and masturbation are discontinued, the body usually reacts with wet dreams.

mechanisms that this activity triggers in a man's body. All of the key steps in this process are described within this book. I also give pointers on how to categorically stop pornography use and masturbation. It will be a lot easier if you become aware of what is happening in your body when you experience a powerful tension and what effects its remission will bring. It's necessary to understand the problem in order to deal with it. In addition, the method I propose will help you not only to ultimately abandon pornography, but also to convert this achievement into an invaluable force that will allow you to attain your most ambitious goals. In the book, I mainly describe how giving up pornography can affect your development and can strengthen the features that will help you to lead a happy life, to reach your goals, and even to get rich. I have also included a number of fundamental questions related to getting rich, which will help you understand the significance of the problem. I have made every effort to ensure that my message is concise and comprehensible, and that the information has been verified and is presented objectively.

It's up to you how you use your potential.

In a few places, I refer to resources, forums, and support groups that will also help you to resist sexual stimuli. Besides, if this book turns out to be insufficient for you, you can explore the subject yourself by referring to these resources. Do not hesitate to pass on this knowledge to any loved ones who are in need.

2. SYSTEM BASICS

> *The doctor of the future will give no medication, but will interest his patients in the care of the human frame, diet and in the cause and prevention of disease.*
>
> - Thomas A. Edison

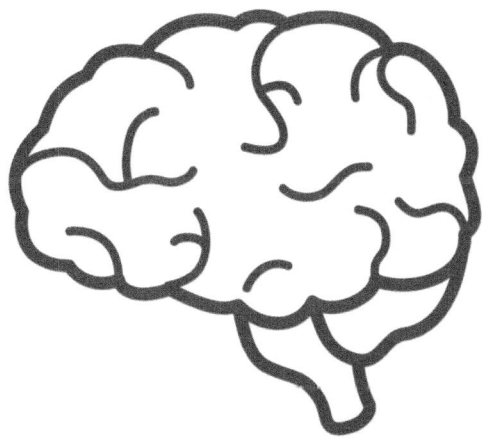

2.1. THE MOST COMMON PROBLEMS

In order for you to properly understand what the problem is, I'll explain how pornography works with masturbation and how they are linked to addiction. One of the people who investigated the porn issue is Gary Wilson, in his book, *Your Brain on Porn*.[6] Wilson also founded a website under the same name. You can find a lot of information there, as well as links to reliable sources. I will try to describe the issue as concisely and as understandably as possible, because it is only one of the problems covered in this book.

I regret that I didn't learn earlier how this process works. At the age of 14, I believed my schoolmates when they said that masturbating to pornography is normal. At first, my suspicion and respect for nudity made me skeptical about pornography. Over time, curiosity and my inability to cope with sexual tension won. It was only years later that I began to deduce that pornography was causing the havoc in my mind and body.

Do any of the following symptoms seem familiar to you?

- a lack of satisfaction and contentment derived from everyday activities or entertainment
- lingering bitterness and a lack of enthusiasm
- neglect of responsibilities and sloppy work performance
- chronic fatigue
- a lack of motivation
- difficulty concentrating and deteriorated short-term memory
- memory problems
- growing social anxiety
- reduced libido
- shyness
- general anxiety or a desire to hide
- irrational fear
- an imagination that often generates sexual images
- constant sexual tension and lack of satisfaction after orgasm

---

[6] https://yourbrainonporn.com

- problems getting/maintaining an erection during intercourse
- problems achieving orgasm during intercourse
- odd pelvic pain
- objectification of women
- the need for stronger and stronger stimuli, more vulgar pornography, and new fetishes

These are some of the possible symptoms of pornography abuse and frequent masturbation. I experienced a number of them after a few months of regularly visiting porn websites. If you habitually masturbate to porn and experience any of these symptoms at the same time, it is a sign that you are doing it too often. If you have not experienced any of these symptoms yet, it is not too late to break the habit without discovering their side effects. Unfortunately, when these symptoms appear—especially the physical ones—the matter becomes serious.

Contemporary medicine is still in its infancy when it comes to dealing with the abuse of sexual stimuli. Only a small group of specialists are aware of the cause of the above-mentioned ailments. Others, who do not know this, refer their patients to psychologists and prescribe various—often unsuitable—medications. They simply cannot help. Only in the past few years has there been widespread access to high-speed internet and free, high-quality pornography. Likewise, it's only been a few years since patients with such problems started visiting their doctors. As a rule, doctors don't know what's going on, and from the beginning they disqualify pornography and masturbation as the cause. Nonetheless, it has been reiterated for many years that masturbation is actually healthy for the male body. It's just that medicine envisions masturbation aided by the imagination or gaudy magazines and grainy video tapes. These media—which are now rarely used—only offer a substitute for the sensations that modern high-quality pornography guarantees.

Before the Internet era, an inquisitive youngster usually soon got bored playing with himself, and was genuinely anticipating his first experiences with women. With the current possibilities offered by the porn industry, and especially by its regular exploration, it is increasingly difficult to deliver enjoyment in any other way. Sadly, this results in a waning attraction to real relationships with the opposite sex or a reduced pleasure from having sex in real life. This is evidenced by a survey[7] carried out in Italy: as many as 10% of the students participating in it admitted that pornography lessened their desire to find a real partner, and 16% of those viewing pornography at least once a week confirmed a decline in desire. There were no such cases among the participants who didn't use pornography.

It often happens (I experienced it myself) that a pornography viewer strives to have sex with a woman more from a sense of male obligation, and less because of his natural instinct. Often, sexual intercourse does not take place because the man has erectile dysfunction.[8] It also turns out that he cannot orgasm inside a woman's vagina, which is not as tight as a clenched fist. It tends to be very unpleasant when you can't satisfy your own desire or your partner's expectations. Similar things happen when you stress yourself out before intercourse. Wanting to rise to the challenge can paralyze you. That is how I explained my weak performances and that's how my partner treated them as well. This is usually the first misdiagnosis when it comes

---

[7] Pizzol D, Bertoldo A, Foresta C (2016): *Adolescents and web porn: a new era of sexuality.*

[8] Brian Y. Park, Gary Wilson, Jonathan Berger, Matthew Christman, Bryn Reina, Frank Bishop, Warren P. Klam and Andrew P. Doan (2016): *Is Internet Pornography Causing Sexual Dysfunctions? A Review with Clinical Reports.*

to watching pornography and masturbation.[9] Believe me, nothing arouses an appetite like hunger. In this case, it's a matter of the central reward system. We are able to get an erection and have sex only thanks to the powerful release of dopamine[10]. A period of abstinence from pornography and sexual arousal can regenerate the receptors in the brain and can allow us to once again become satisfied with the normal doses of dopamine secreted before or during intercourse with a woman. Fortunately, giving up pornography for some time can help.[11] For some it may take one month, for others perhaps one year—but the detox usually works. The first evidence indicates that the longer someone has used porn and the higher quality it was, the longer the detox period will take.

2.2. HOW IT WORKS

The cause of the disorders described above is several mechanisms related to watching pornography. One of them is known as the Coolidge effect.[12] It is named after the American president, Calvin Coolidge. According to an anecdote, the president and his wife were visiting a chicken farm. When the president's wife learned that the rooster

---

[9] Simone Kühn, Jürgen Gallinat (2014): *Brain Structure and Functional Connectivity Associated With Pornography Consumption: The Brain on Porn.*

[10] To be clear, dopamine is part of the "pleasure cascade." It is more about the anticipation of reward, the motivation to seek it. The feeling of reward itself comes from endogenous opioids. I encourage you to investigate the topic more.

[11] Bronner G, Ben-Zion IZ (2014): *Unusual masturbatory practice as an etiological factor in the diagnosis and treatment of sexual dysfunction in young men.*

[12] Wikipedia: *Coolidge Effect.*

could mate dozens of times a day, she told the attendant to repeat this to President Coolidge. When the news about roosters' sexual potential was passed on to him, the president asked if these dozens of sexual relations happened with the same hen each time. When he heard that this wasn't the case, he asked the attendant to tell that to Mrs. Coolidge...

The best illustration of this mechanism is an experiment in which a male rat and a female rat are placed in a cage. It is easy to predict that the male rat will be eager to start mating with the female. After the first intercourse, he will be a bit weary, and in the following approaches he will need more time to ejaculate or he will become completely uninterested in this female. Everything starts all over again when the female is swapped for a new one. Then the male regains his vigor and tries to impregnate the new female. This substitution of females can be continued until the male is physically exhausted. The appearance of a new female increases dopamine levels, stimulating the reward system. This primitive mechanism also works in humans; its aim is to encourage us to reproduce and to conceive as many children as possible. Unfortunately, it also works when a man's brain sees a naked woman on a computer screen. When a man constantly sees the same woman, the brain quickly gets bored and the level of dopamine drops. In these times of high-speed Internet and access to millions of movies featuring different women, it's possible to maintain a consistently high level of dopamine. Watching pornography, particularly a series of new videos with new women, leads to sustained high levels of dopamine. This mechanism causes the viewer to become easily addicted to the constant hits of dopamine. Thanks to the free access to porn content and the minimum effort needed to obtain a constant flow of dopamine, the reward system becomes more and more resistant to low doses of dopamine, and after a while only new pornography can cause it to spike.

A significant factor in this mechanism is novelty, for

which the reward system triggers the discharge of dopamine. Because the system rewards you for new experiences, we fondly remember the first time we engage in various activities. This is also one of the reasons why surfing the web is so engaging. Internet resources provide an endless supply of novelties. Another woman to copulate with is also another novelty. The combination of discovering new experiences and watching pornography creates a huge surge of dopamine levels.[13] Australian scientists have conducted a study[14] in which a man was shown the same part of an erotic film over and over again. With each successive screening, his sexual arousal subsided. When another movie was played, his arousal immediately increased. It's easy to guess that a brain which has just seen dozens of naked women within a few minutes on the Internet is unlikely to be permanently stimulated by one real-life woman. The dopamine influx won't be powerful enough to act on the reproductive organs.

The primitive reward system has evolved to propel us towards survival. This system rewards us with dopamine for food, reproduction, love, achievements, friendship, and novelty. The higher the dopamine production is during a given activity, the more we desire it. As a result, if something does not grant an adequate hit of dopamine, then naturally, we are not interested in it. Sexual activity is the greatest possible source of a natural dopamine hit for the brain. Dopamine also plays a key role in drug addiction, as drugs constitute an unnatural source of vast surges of dopamine in the body. The mechanisms of addiction to pornography and drugs are similar. After taking drugs (e.g.,

---

[13] Paula Banca, Laurel S. Morris, Simon Mitchell, Neil A. Harrison, Marc N. Potenza, Valerie Voon (2015): *Novelty, conditioning and attentional bias to sexual rewards*.

[14] Koukounas E, Over R (2000): *Changes in the magnitude of the eyeblink startle response during habituation of sexual arousal*.

amphetamines or cocaine) dopamine transporters become inhibited, that is, the body struggles to remove the dopamine from between the neurons.[15] This intensifies the action of dopamine on its receptors. In consequence, a person feels as euphoric as when he or she achieves something, such as winning a difficult competition or even having sexual intercourse. However, the accumulation of large doses of dopamine destroys some of the receptors, and the brain becomes desensitized to smaller amounts of dopamine, which can lead to feeling down in the dumps.

Lower doses of narcotics stimulate the feeling of an energy boost, heightened motivation, and enhanced cognitive abilities. This is because dopamine is not just connected with rewards. It is also responsible for our pursuit of a reward, our anticipation, and desire. Dopamine spurs incentive motivation; this is what pushes us to achieve long-term objectives and win potential prizes. When we are striving for a goal, small doses of dopamine are secreted naturally. Thanks to that, we become focused, our senses are sharpened, and our muscles can do more than usual. The motivational feature of the reward system is essential for achieving happiness and satisfaction. If we want to pursue those aims, we need to take care of this system, especially in these days of such powerful, readily-available stimuli. When the reward system is abused, we may not even feel those small doses of dopamine which are crucial for motivation, so our damaged dopamine receptors may need more of it to cause a similar effect. This is also why some people are addicted to sources of high dopamine spikes, such as drugs.

Relationships with women are a very good example of how natural motivation is built through the reward system. When we meet an attractive woman, the brain triggers a

---

[15] National Institute on Drug Abuse (2016): *How does cocaine produce its effects?*; BBC Three (2011): *How does cocaine affect the brain? - How drugs work, Cocaine, Preview*.

small rush of dopamine, which increases our level of motivation. This motivation encourages us to approach the woman, talk to her, impress her, and invite her somewhere. This motivation also means that we want to maintain this acquaintance and eventually establish a lasting relationship. The next stages of the relationship with this woman drive the flow of even larger infusions of dopamine, causing excitement,[16] while sexual intercourse with her triggers a burst of dopamine leading to euphoria. Note, however, that advertisements with women in their underwear also provoke excitement, and that interacting with pornography very quickly incites euphoria. Pornography viewers often give up relationships with real women because they know that pornography will deliver the euphoria much faster.

STIMULUS EXAMPLE	DOPAMINE	REACTION
Attractive woman	●●●●●●	Motivation
Woman in lingerie, erotization, touching, kissing	●●●●●●●●●●●●	Excitation
Naked body, pornography, sexual intercourse	●●●●●●●●●●●●●●●●●●●●●●●●	Euphoria

Pornography also changes attitudes towards women and makes it difficult to establish a healthy relationship. Lamentably, one's natural interest in everyday relationships

---

[16] Perhaps the dopamine effect is also responsible for feelings and love.

with women can be impaired by eroticization and pornography. Pornography objectifies women. As a result, the only thing that we come to expect from them is the rush from a large dose of dopamine. Women sense our intentions straightaway and perceive our behavior as incomprehensible or inappropriate. Unfortunately, constant virtual encounters with sexual stimuli anesthetize the reward system, a system that is based on small amounts of dopamine which are necessary for creating the motivation needed to maintain a normal relationship and finding a partner.

Remember, the motivational rationale of the reward system is necessary to achieve fulfillment in life. We need motivation in order to work, learn, find ideas, build businesses, and to set life goals and realize them. It is not worth forfeiting such an important driving force of the body for temporary pleasures in the form of artificial stimuli.[17] You might wonder how it's possible, then, that some people with a high social status or substantial wealth lead a promiscuous life, and liberally use stimulants and the sex industry. The answer is simple: typically, these people already have flourishing businesses and have achieved their status thanks to their previous work or inheritance. It may be that their image helps them to get richer. In most cases, however, to build capital from scratch, you need unlimited levels of motivation, inner strength, and years of hard work that cannot be ruined by momentary pleasures.

Now you know why a reward system which is fatigued by pornography does not motivate you to succeed. What's worse, when we reach for artificial stimuli, we subconsciously form a mental pattern, leading ourselves to believe that any other actions or efforts will not provide us with so much pleasure so easily. On the other hand, the

---

[17] Simone Kühn, PhD, Jürgen Gallinat, PhD (2014): *Brain Structure and Functional Connectivity Associated With Pornography Consumption: The Brain on Porn.*

good news is that abused dopamine receptors should regenerate after a certain period of abstinence from strong stimuli, which will allow the reward system to return to normal.

2.3. SUPERNORMAL STIMULI

In 1973, Nikolaas Tinbergen received the Nobel Prize in Physiology or Medicine for a series of extraordinary discoveries regarding the factors that govern animal behavior.[18] He discovered, for example, that if a bird who lays distinctive eggs has her own egg substituted with a larger, but similar egg, she will brood more eagerly than atop her own. The choice of egg is instinctive. A larger egg with more strongly pronounced characteristics of the given species may indicate that the chick will be stronger when hatched and will have a better chance of survival. Such a biological adaptation of the species seems to make sense. However, Tinbergen continued the experiment, placing ever-larger dummy eggs into the bird's nest. It turned out that there was almost no limit to the increase in stimulus that the bird would respond to. Birds were even trying to brood eggs that would have been physically impossible for them to lay. It didn't bother them when the eggs were nearly as big as the birds themselves and they would slip off their surface. Taking into account that the birds chose large plaster eggs at the expense of their real offspring, one might suppose that this mechanism is defective. What Tinbergen developed is called the supernormal stimulus. This is a stimulus whose effect on instinctive behavior is directly proportional to the level of its exaggeration. Supernormal stimuli even work when they are so strong that they do not occur naturally in such a form. They impact our behavior more effectively than anything else, so we often desire fake things more than real ones.

---

[18] Wikipedia: *Supenormal Stimulus*

The basic proof that humans are also susceptible to supernormal stimuli are sweets and fatty foods. Prehistoric people did not have such comfortable living conditions and such easy access to food as we do now, so sugar and fat became a very strong stimulus for collecting food and obtaining energy. When the characteristics of the human body were developing, people didn't know about agriculture or animal husbandry. Fruits rich in sugar and vitamins were hard to come by and could only be found when in season. Wild animals—which were not easy to catch—had almost no fat, in contrast to those bred today. Unfortunately, these stimuli have been exploited by the industry in order to sell junk food. People often stuff themselves with unhealthy food, although they are aware of the danger. This demonstrates how susceptible the human brain is to supernormal stimuli. Marketing research even indicates that the more sugar a product has, the higher its sales are.

Unfortunately, people have learned how to use supernormal incentives for commercial purposes. The same is true for the human body. There are ubiquitous advertisements featuring beautiful and often semi-naked people. Using the human body to promote products often completely unconnected with the body has for a long time exceeded the limits of logic. The pornography industry openly uses this mechanism. Even the sight of a naked body is a very strong stimulus for a man. All you need is easy access and minor suggestions for the man to swallow the hook and ogle the pictures and videos. However, pornographers went even further. They took the most intense stimuli of human sexuality and exaggerated them to unnatural proportions. Porn actors have strongly accentuated sexual characteristics, and their interactions, speed of movement, and positions have little to do with natural sex. Unfortunately, we easily succumb to sexual stimuli, so we can quickly become addicted to commonly available pornography. The fact that people often choose pornography over dating and sex proves that pornography is an artificial, supernormal stimulus.

2.4. CHEMICALS AND HORMONES

Watching pornography and masturbating frequently wreak havoc in both the mind and the body. As is wellknown, each act of masturbation leads to ejaculation and a loss of sperm. When we lose sperm, the body begins to rebuild its supply. Semen is the most capital-intensive tissue that the male body produces. The more often we lose it, the more energy the body spends on its production. The production of spermatozoa, which are components of the sperm, is based on spermatogenesis and is time-consuming: it takes approximately 70 days.[19] A large part of the process involves duplicating the genetic code and multiplying it. The ejaculate itself consists of valuable vitamins and minerals that are collected from the entire body. It is made up of enzymes, proteins, amino acids, flavonoids, zinc, selenium, and vitamin C. Most of the chemicals necessary to create a new supply of sperm are also needed for the proper functioning of other organs. If these components are excessively used to produce ejaculate, the body may become deficient in them. A single ejaculation can cause a slight fatigue of the body, whereas frequent ejaculation can result in a deficiency of micronutrients and vitamins, and even faintness.

The loss of semen alone, however, does not affect the mood and well-being of a man as it does the hormone economy associated with it. The common understanding is that frequent ejaculation has a negative effect on libido.

---

[19] Although the whole process takes 2–3 months, spermatogenesis takes place continuously, so each ejaculation reduces the number of "ready sperm." It is estimated that the fourth ejaculation in a 12-hour period contains a negligible number of spermatozoa.
Gilbert SF (2000): *Developmental Biology. 6th edition*

This issue was first described by Sigmund Freud. He defined libido as the internal energy through which "the drives of life" fulfill their functions. Considering the time period—the end of the 19th century—his observations were quite accurate. Libido can also be described as the attitude toward and mental representation of the inner sex drive.

It is often assumed that a high libido signifies a man who feels comfortable in the company of women and that it is connected with self-confidence, but—in my opinion—self-confidence has more to do with undertaking challenges, being competitive, taking risks, or being a leader. In the case of libido and sexual relations with women, we should say that we feel at ease, and that our relationships are natural and healthy. The term "self-confidence" can equate relationships with women to the achievement of a goal and its objectification. This approach seems unhealthy and can have destructive effects on a man and his relationships with women. Why should these relationships be raised to the level of an achievement? Why focus on something that is natural and results from innate instincts? Unfortunately, analyzing and conniving ways to seduce a woman does not help with libido. This behavior is typical of pornography fans who replace natural behavior with plotting about "how to get into her pants." We definitely make a better impression and achieve better results when we stop thinking, or even turn off our intellect and rely on nature. It is true that men with high libido—who are comfortable in the company of women—receive more attention from the opposite sex. Women can easily sense who behaves naturally around them and who does not. Interestingly, this natural male behavior is determined to a large extent by variables such as hormones.

Testosterone, which is also responsible for the development of masculine features, principally influences libido. Its production occurs chiefly in the testes and to a small extent in the adrenal glands as well. It plays a decisive role during sexual maturation, and in the development and growth of the sex organs. It also helps to build and maintain bone density, to increase muscle mass and strength, and to break down fat. It stimulates the production of red blood cells and semen. Thanks to testosterone, we feel confident, strong, level-headed, and calm; we easily cope with stressful situations and can manage risk. Testosterone kindles the need to discover and explore the world. There is a direct dependence, meaning that a high level of testosterone implies increased exploratory activity. In animals, this is manifested by an active examination of the surrounding environment and the objects found within. In humans, it takes the form of cognitive curiosity. Testosterone is essential in a man's life.

It is easy to conclude that if a large amount of testosterone is consumed, for example, by ejaculation and sperm production, testosterone levels may decrease. However, research suggests that masturbation does not significantly affect blood testosterone levels before, during, or after masturbation. At the moment of a masturbation-induced orgasm, testosterone levels are relatively stable, and large amounts of noradrenaline, adrenaline, and prolactin are released into the bloodstream.[20] It is only in the case of regular masturbation that normal testosterone levels may decrease. For ethical reasons, testosterone levels have not been checked before and after regular masturbation. We know, however, that limiting masturbation in the long run results in an upsurge of normal testosterone levels. This was studied by scientists from Essen,[21] who checked testosterone levels 3 weeks after the

---

[20] Exton NG, Truong TC, Exton MS, Wingenfeld SA, Leygraf N, Saller B, Hartmann U, Schedlowski M. (2000): *Neuroendocrine response to film-induced sexual arousal in men and women.*

[21] Exton MS, Krüger TH, Bursch N, Haake P, Knapp W, Schedlowski M, Hartmann U (2001): *Endocrine response to masturbation-induced orgasm in healthy men following a 3-week sexual abstinence.*

last masturbation-induced orgasm. The results were unambiguous: "higher testosterone levels were observed after a period of abstinence." Why does this happen? The reason for falling testosterone levels may be a deficiency of the micronutrients which are necessary to produce testosterone[22]—for example, zinc and selenium—and which masturbating too often can flush out of the body. Testosterone production is a complex process that requires a lot of valuable compounds to be supplied by the body. Another reason may be prolactin, which is responsible for about 300 different processes. In men, an elevated prolactin level also lowers testosterone production, so maintaining an elevated prolactin level for a longer time—through frequent masturbation, for example—can reduce testosterone levels. Prolactin is responsible for the feeling of satiation after intercourse, but a masturbation-induced orgasm causes a much smaller amount to be secreted.[23] On the other hand, prolactin levels after sex are higher than after masturbation, though they drop faster. Masturbation does not allow you to become satiated after sexual stimulation to the same extent as sex does, so you can assume that when this cycle is often repeated, elevated prolactin levels are sustained in the body. One cause of decreased libido[24] is a sharp decrease in androgen receptors (i.e., testosterone receptors) in the hypothalamus due to masturbating too frequently. The

---

[22] Scott I Zeitlin, MD and Jacob Rajfer, MD (2000): *Hyperprolactinemia and Erectile Dysfunction.*

[23] Brody S, Krüger TH (2006): *The post-orgasmic prolactin increase following intercourse is greater than following masturbation and suggests greater satiety*;
John M. Grohol, Psy.D. (2006): *Orgasms Best in Sex vs. Masturbation.*

[24] Romano-Torres M, Phillips-Farfán BV, Chavira R, Rodríguez-Manzo G, Fernández-Guasti A. (2007): *Relationship between sexual satiety and brain androgen receptors.*

result is that the body stops feeling the presence of testosterone and we start behaving as if we don't have enough of it.

Interestingly, some studies have indicated that relations with women and having sex with a partner have a major impact on raising testosterone levels. In one study,[25] 42 men were sent to a sex club; 26 of them had sex and the rest only observed the situation. The group that had sex had increased their testosterone levels by about 70%, while the men who only watched sexual activity experienced increases of just over 10%. In another study,[26] the testosterone levels of the men in 4 couples were measured before and after sex in the evening, as well as the following day when the couples did not have sex. This study showed that testosterone levels went up when intercourse occurred, but remained at the same level before sex and after nights without sex. Based on these studies, it can be concluded that sexual intercourse with a woman has an influence on increased testosterone levels in a man, and even that successful intercourse contributes to this increase. Perhaps this is caused by the mere fact of satisfying a woman and the feeling of fulfilling the role of a male. Another factor may be female pheromones. The studied effect of women's presence on testosterone levels in men allows us to assume that normal levels of testosterone are lower in men who do not plan to interact with women for a long time. This applies mainly to men who watch pornography and regularly masturbate in solitude, and to those who don't but have abandoned relationships with women, perhaps because of insecurities.

Lowered testosterone levels cause a lack of confidence,

---

[25] Michelle J. Escasa, Jacqueline F. Casey, Peter B. Gray (2011): *Salivary Testosterone Levels in Men at a U.S. Sex Club*.

[26] Dabbs JM Jr, Mohammed S (1992): *Male and female salivary testosterone concentrations before and after sexual activity*.

a feeling of less masculinity, fearfulness, and sociopathy. Men with low levels of testosterone often have soft bones, poorly developed muscle tissue, obesity, a greater tendency for gynecomastia (breast formation), an increased risk of cardiovascular disease, higher levels of bad cholesterol (LDL), and neurological and psychological problems.[27] On the other hand, excessive testosterone levels may cause bald spots, faster development of an enlarged prostate, lower good cholesterol levels (HDL), or fits of aggression. However, radically elevating and maintaining testosterone levels without medication is not as easy as reducing them. On the Internet, you can find many tips on how to slightly boost your testosterone level, e.g., by eating a proper diet, getting enough sleep, taking cold showers, or just finding a girlfriend. Remember that an imbalance of the male hormonal system can lead to unpleasant consequences. Frequent masturbation can mean lower testosterone levels or an impaired response to testosterone in the body, and living with limited testosterone can be difficult or even risky for a man.

Sexual experiences are the most intense natural stimulus of the reward system for people. Pornography helps us to cheat our brains and to enjoy endless sexual pleasure. Pornography makes it easier to get a powerful injection of dopamine and to masturbate, bringing orgasms sooner. It also enables us to increase the frequency of orgasms over time, as opposed to sexual intercourse with one partner. However, it makes it harder to be satiated. A man's body is naturally equipped with a mechanism of rest after sexual contact, allowing it to regenerate. As I mentioned before, an extraordinary amount of prolactin is secreted after a sexual act,[28] thanks to which a man feels sated and

---

[27] Tylka, T. L. (2015): *No harm in looking, right? Men's pornography consumption, body image, and well-being.*

[28] Wikipedia: *Prolactin*

gratified. This is meant to counter the depressive effect of overloading the dopamine receptors. The inflow of large doses of dopamine during stimulation and orgasm are a drain on the reward system, which may result in feelings of dejection and disappointment during other activities. However, it should be noted that the amount of prolactin secreted after sex is up to 400% higher than the rise in prolactin after masturbation.[29] Additionally, each subsequent masturbation occurring within a short time is very likely to trigger a smaller and smaller release of prolactin. If the amount of the secreted prolactin is smaller and smaller, each following masturbation elicits more and more depression. Unfortunately, the feeling of depression can also lead to addiction.[30] As a matter of fact, depression is one of the main reasons why people develop addictions. This is because the human brain also works defensively when we are in a bad mood and feeling downhearted. In these cases, the brain suggests returning to the last activity that made us feel better. It is not hard to guess that if this activity was masturbating to pornography, then the brain will push us to return to it—all the more so because access to innumerable new pornographic films provides unending stimulation. This creates a vicious circle of addiction.

The reward system and the endocrine system, especially dopamine and testosterone, play a key role in a man's life. Watching pornography and frequently masturbating can contribute to an imbalance in these systems, and thus of the body and of the functioning of the brain. This, in turn, can ruin your motivation, deprive you of pleasure from

---

[29] Brody S, Krüger TH (2005): *The post-orgasmic prolactin increase following intercourse is greater than following masturbation and suggests greater satiety.*

[30] Christian Laier, Matthias Brand (2017): *Mood changes after watching pornography on the Internet are linked to tendencies towards Internet-pornography-viewing disorder.*

everyday things, lower your self-confidence, and even limit your opportunities—in your personal life, in your search for a life partner, in your dreams, in raising your qualifications, in pursuing success, and in getting rich.

2.5. WHERE DO WE BEGIN

There is a certain age bracket in the development of a man in which his life's paths crystallize. Most often, it is during puberty and early adulthood. In these stages, we particularly devote ourselves to getting an education, gaining experience, shaping our personality, and increasing our potential. It is very important to allow the body to develop in a healthy, unhindered way. Particularly in this period, intense stimuli may contribute to an abnormal growth of the brain and other organs. It is during adolescence that doing sports and pursuing cultural and scientific interests is imperative for one's future career. Our first demanding experiences at this age strengthen our character, develop our intellectual skills, and make us resistant to stress and risk in adulthood. Schools and local communities offer unlimited opportunities to develop one's passions. However, all of this may seem dull and uninteresting if other strong stimuli appear before the young mind.

The discovery of one's sexuality is often accompanied by masturbation. It shouldn't be harmful if done in moderation, and after a while, playing with yourself will simply become boring. Pornography can successfully engage you for longer, though. Frequent masturbation combined with pornography can disrupt the natural process of development. I remember from my own experience that from the moment I started to watch pornography, I abandoned my passion for sports and music. Before these artificial stimuli appeared in my life, I would step onto the court or field wanting to become the best, and at school I studied hard. When I started to regularly dedicate my time to pornography, that zeal instantly disappeared.[31] I became lazy and disobedient. I didn't see the point in anything. Nothing made me happy. My motivation evaporated. I degenerated from earning very good grades to being an average student. My education consisted only in passing from year to year, so as not to disappoint my parents. The world around me seemed gray and gloomy.[32] I believed that somewhere else there was a better place where everything looked different, but where I was things were lousy and I didn't have to try. I had a constant sense of discontentment with everything. It accompanied me practically everywhere I went, among friends, at school, and with my family. Now I don't like being around such bitter people, but I used to be that way myself. And it all happened during the years that were supposed to be the most beautiful and blissful, and which I was supposed to pine for as an adult.

Unfortunately, my abused reward system was unable to provide me the joy of everyday life. Before I started habitually watching pornography, I was brave. I started many projects and engaged others in them. When I started to watch porn, my courage vanished.[33] I avoided any risky situations. I even avoided using public transport and leaving the house alone. The prolonged time my body went

---

[31] Boies SC, Cooper A, Osborne CS (2004): *Variations in internet-related problems and psychosocial functioning in online sexual activities: implications for social and sexual development of young adults.*

[32] Weaver JB 3rd, Weaver SS, Mays D, Hopkins GL, Kannenberg W, McBride D (2010): *Mental- and physical-health indicators and sexually explicit media use behavior by adults.*

[33] Valerie Voon, Thomas B. Mole, Paula Banca, Laura Porter, Laurel Morris, Simon Mitchell, Tatyana R. Lapa, Judy Karr, Neil A. Harrison, Marc N. Potenza, Michael Irvine (2014): *Neural Correlates of Sexual Cue Reactivity in Individuals with and without Compulsive Sexual Behaviours.*

without the correct amount of testosterone meant that my functioning was limited.

Before pornography appeared in my life, I had a lot of female friends and acquaintances who I was happy to hang out with.[34] Our relationships were based on mutual respect and trust. Pornography, however, taught me to look for an advantage in every friendship with a girl.[35] Before, the girls liked me and I didn't treat them objectively. Later, I began to pay attention only to their appearance, and I considered old friendships to be a waste of time. Spending time with girls was now a mission to get to the next base.[36] The paradox was that my focused sex drive was a kind of tension that could never be satisfied. My dealings in love became caricatures, because my relationships with girls didn't provide me with any joy; I only took part out of a sense of duty. These relationships were so ridiculous because my libido was constantly being rebuilt. Inside, I felt anxious and maybe even timid: I became shy, which made it challenging for me to meet new people.[37] As you can easily guess, such relationships cannot be maintained. From online forums, I know that a lot of pornography users complain of nervousness and social anxiety. As a young man, I was unaware of where it came from. After all, it seemed like everything was under control. To make matters

---

[34] Andreas G. Philaretou, Ahmed Y. Mahfouz, Katherine R. Allen (2005): *Use of Internet Pornography and Men's Well-Being*.

[35] Kasper TE, Short MB, Milam AC. (2014): *Narcissism and Internet pornography use*.

[36] Walton MT, Cantor JM, Lykins AD (2015): *An Online Assessment of Personality, Psychological, and Sexuality Trait Variables Associated with Self-Reported Hypersexual Behavior*.

[37] Stephanie S. Luster, Larry J. Nelson, Franklin O. Poulsen, Brian J. Willoughby (2013): *Emerging Adult Sexual Attitudes and Behaviors: Does Shyness Matter?*

worse, more and more people were talking about how harmless masturbation is, which encouraged me to use pornography and prevented me from attributing any consequences to it.

I can't turn back time or predict how my life would have gone if I hadn't clicked on a pornography website and hadn't been fooled by these strong stimuli. I realize, however, that life goes on and I can still make up for lost time. All that remains is the regret that I spent a large part of my teenage years watching porn actors copulating.

3. WHAT HAS BEEN SEEN CANNOT BE UNSEEN

*You've got one body and one mind—
that's all that is really yours. This body
and this mind feel fine now, but they have
to last you a lifetime.*

3.1. REMEMBERING

The power of the human mind lies in a very good memory and a vivid imagination. It's good that we remember the beautiful moments from our lives. We can always lift our spirits by conjuring pleasant memories. However, our memory also records things we would like to forget about. People say that it is hard to put your past behind you. It is usually difficult, especially a short time after the event. With time, though, it is easier to forget about certain things because we can distance ourselves from what happened. We also subconsciously erase unpleasant experiences from our memory.

In the case of pornography, it would be much better if we did not remember the scenes and characters we watch. Pornography is easily evoked by human memory, and this can have a very damaging effect on the body. Pornographic thoughts can contribute to a rise in sexual tension, due to which you cannot function normally. If we induce sexual arousal in ourselves, for example when we are in class or at work, we are not able to focus on our activities or perform them assiduously. We cannot concentrate on studying and when we have a job to do, we either procrastinate or do it sloppily in order to carry on thinking about naked women and to release the tension. Additionally, when we recall erotic images in our memory, the body subconsciously prepares itself for sexual intercourse. This brings about sexual arousal and activates the reproductive organs, which begin to produce the ingredients of the ejaculate. If we often generate arousal in ourselves and we don't relieve the sexual tension by ejaculating, unpleasant feelings may appear in the pelvis and testicles.

Unfortunately, pornographic images are the most difficult for the brain to erase from memory. The brain associates these images with something that was pleasant. What's more, it recalls these pictures very quickly and accurately. Sometimes, pornography fans are not only unable to get rid of the images and movies in their memory, but are also unable to stop involuntarily conjuring up these images. Pornography is not only about watching: it is also thinking about pornography, remembering, and imagining. Watching pornography can play a part in the deterioration of memory, and more specifically, it can make it difficult to remember other important information. The brain scrupulously records what is pleasurable and intense for it, and if something does not cause such pleasure or is not intense enough, the brain will be reluctant to remember it.

3.2. RESEARCH ON BRAIN PERFORMANCE

A German study[38] suggested that a man becomes forgetful when looking at erotic pictures. The subject of the study was short-term memory, which is necessary for carrying out tasks, understanding issues, and making deductions and decisions. Twenty-eight men at a mean age of 26 were given memory tasks to solve, but before doing so, some of them were shown erotic pictures while others were shown photos of ordinary, everyday activities. The men who looked at erotic pictures achieved an average score of 67% correct answers, whereas those in the second group got an average of 80% correct. This study showed that sexual arousal triggered by erotic images conflicted with the efficiency of working memory and caused the brain to disregard information coming from the environment. This increased the number of wrong decisions. It is interesting that people who rated the pictures as not very stimulating had a greater need for masturbation and scored lower in the task which tested their working memory. The authors of the study found that sexual arousal and its impact on cognitive processes may explain some of these negative effects.

Other studies have shown that sexual stimuli also impact executive functions. They demonstrated that sexual stimulation negatively affects our reaction time,[39] target

---

[38] Laier C, Schulte FP, Brand M (2012): *Pornographic picture processing interferes with working memory performance.*

[39] Lester W. Wright Jr., Henry E. Adams (2010): *The effects of stimuli that vary in erotic content on cognitive processes.*

perception,[40] and decision-making.[41] They also investigated how watching pornography influences adolescents.[42] It turned out that frequent use of adult content results in a deterioration of learning ability.

The researchers Ariely and Loewenstein emphasize that sex drive is an important force which affects our behavior.[43] Their study revealed that sexual arousal largely correlates with a person's judgment and decision-making. Subjects who were sexually stimulated were more likely to engage in diverse sexual activities that were not perceived as desirable when they were not sexually aroused. This finding refutes the view that sexual preferences are an individual characteristic, as they are triggered by situations, not by decisions. Moreover, the researchers showed that men are more likely to violate ethical rules in order to satisfy their sexual appetites. When the brain receives a signal that there is an opportunity for intercourse, the willingness to have sex increases automatically.

People who often watch pornography exhibit hypersexuality, or excessive sexual appetite.[44] It is typical for such people that any sexual stimuli encountered in reality or recalled from memory—even ambiguous stimuli

---

[40] Steven B. Most, Stephen D. Smith , Amy B. Cooter , Bethany N. Levy, David H. Zald (2007): *The naked truth: Positive, arousing distractors impair rapid target perception.*

[41] Laier C, Pawlikowski M, Brand M (2014): *Sexual picture processing interferes with decision-making under ambiguity.*

[42] Beyens I., Vandenbosch L., Eggermont S. (2015): *Early adolescent boys' exposure to Internet pornography: Relationships to pubertal timing, sensation seeking, and academic performance.*

[43] Dan Ariely George Loewenstein (2005): *The heat of the moment: the effect of sexual arousal on sexual decision making.*

[44] S.Kühn, J.Gallinat (2016): *Chapter Three - Neurobiological Basis of Hypersexuality.*

or sexual innuendo—give rise to sexual tension and arousal. Such people are much more exposed to the weakening of cognitive abilities and limited self-control resulting from sexual desire.

Personally, I once participated in a study conducted as part of the master's thesis of a psychology student of a large university. When I was in college, before I started earning an income, I often had the opportunity to earn pocket money. The study's warnings about the risk of viewing adult material did not deter me, because at that time I was using it almost daily. Neither before nor during the test did I know what its purpose was. I was given a series of quite difficult logical tasks to complete. They consisted of choosing the best solution to a problem that needed to be recalculated. I wanted to achieve the best result possible because the best score would earn an additional prize. In cases where I had doubts, it took me a long time to choose the correct answer. When I solved the first puzzles, I was presented with a series of pornographic images, which I had to assess on a scale of 1 to 7. After looking at the photos, I was given a second series of similar logical tasks. These tasks were not any more difficult, but the calculations became so demanding that I could hardly finish them. In the first series, I did most of the calculations in my head, but in the second series, even with the help of my notes I didn't know what to compare with what in order to form an equation. I solved the initial set of problems by means of calculations, but in the second one, I chose most of my answers intuitively. Honestly, finding the solutions was so difficult for me that I just wanted the test to end.

When I finished, I couldn't wait to ask the researcher about the purpose of the study. I was sure that it was to assess one's weakened math skills, deteriorated short-term memory, and worsened decision-making as a result of sexual arousal. This, however, would have been too obvious. The researcher said that it didn't matter whether I solved the problems correctly. The subject of the study was the amount of time I spent making a decision. It turned out that as a result of sexual arousal I made decisions almost twice as fast! I began to guess the answers to not only those tasks I couldn't figure out, but also for those where calculations could have provided a clear answer. In most of the tasks I just picked a random answer. I would immediately become impatient and marking the correct answer ceased to be so important for me. My motivation to achieve the goal disappeared. In everyday life, such behavior would be extremely irresponsible. Take, for example, people in management positions, who are in charge of their company's success. Exposure to sexual stimuli can affect the quality of their decisions, and thus lead to a decline in the effectiveness of the company they manage.

To sum up, exposing yourself to erotic stimuli and watching pornography may degrade your ability to remember, learn, react, solve problems, and decide. This is due to many factors:
- the disappearance of your motivation to learn,
- the unwillingness to remember boring and low-key events,
- distractions caused by sexual arousal and by pornographic memories popping into your head,
- the focus on sexual satisfaction alone,
- the weakening of your cognitive abilities,
- the deterioration of your short-term memory, and
- the impatience and inclination to put instant gratification before long-term, valuable goals.

3.3. PHYSICAL CHANGES IN THE BRAIN

All of the cognitive and executive limitations related to watching pornography that are described above are reflected in the structure and functioning of the cerebral cortex, mainly in the areas related to the reward system.[45] The brain is an extremely flexible organ of the human body that changes throughout a person's life according to the behavior of its owner.[46] A Berlin study[47] on the response of the brain to sexual signals showed a negative correlation between the amount of time spent watching pornography and the number of gray cells in the stratium—in particular the right caudate and its functional connectivity with the left putamen. This connectivity disorder has also been reported in heroin addicts. The right caudate plays an important role in learning, storing, and processing memorized information.[48] It works like a processor, interpreting the collected data to aid in making decisions and taking future actions. Another study[49] on the reactivity of particular parts of the brain to signals of different sexual content showed a large variation among respondents diagnosed with compulsive sexual behavior (CSB, which also demonstrates hypersexuality, including the frequent use of pornography and masturbation) and those without such a diagnosis. People diagnosed with CSB showed much more desire, while the preferences for the content they watched did not differ from those of people without CSB. An increased desire was associated with the

---

[45] Wikipedia: *Reward system*

[46] Wikipedia: *Neuroplasticity*

[47] Simone Kühn, PhD; Jürgen Gallinat, PhD (2014): *Brain Structure and Functional Connectivity Associated With Pornography Consumption The Brain on Porn.*

[48] Wikipedia: *Caudate nucleus*

[49] Voon V, Mole TB, Banca P, Porter L, Morris L, Mitchell S, Lapa TR, Karr J, Harrison NA, Potenza MN, Irvine M (2014): *Neural correlates of sexual cue reactivity in individuals with and without compulsive sexual behaviours.*

activation of the dorsal anterior cingulate, the ventral striatum, and the amygdala. Such a variance was also found in a study on addiction among drug users. Drug addicts responded to drug-related signals in much the same way as hypersexual people respond to sexual signals. The research I've cited so far has included the most important studies on this matter. I encourage you to study the science of the human brain yourself and to familiarize yourself with a number of other studies on the impact of pornography on the brain.[50]

The above-quoted studies indicate two main disorders in the brain of a person viewing pornography: firstly, an overused reward system that does not react to less-than-intense stimuli and is even limited in function by the atrophy of gray cells in this part of the brain, and secondly, hypersensitivity to sexual signals that prematurely arouse lust and the need to relieve sexual tension. The coexistence of these dysfunctions effectively discourages viewers of pornography from activities other than watching pornography and masturbating, and also weakens their executive function and cognitive control. Thus, as you can see, the lessening of entrepreneurial abilities caused by watching pornography is also causes by physical changes in the brain of the porn viewer.

3.4. THE BRAIN IN ACTION

In order for the mind to nurture the pursuit of ambitious goals, you cannot expose it to weakness or litter it with unnecessary information. Although there is no limit to the amount of knowledge that we can acquire, the content of acquired information can be destructive. Personally, I can confirm—like many people on online forums—that

---

[50] The most important research has been collected here:
https://www.yourbrainonporn.com/brain-scan-studies-porn-users

abandoning pornography gave me clearer thinking, removed mental fog, and increased my patience, efficiency, creativity, speed of thinking, and memory. These are valuable benefits. It is also important to learn to control your thoughts and to not allow the mind to evoke pornographic memories or erotic ideas. Clearing the pornography from your memory completely will be very difficult and almost impossible. Almost everyone still remembers watching their first pornography film, experienced even at a very young age. Over time, after a period of abstinence, memories will slightly fade, and at the same time, the power to control what appears in your mind will definitely increase.

Pornography severely reduces our mental performance. The essence of all projects and businesses is good decision-making, which can be diminished as a result of watching pornography. Making good decisions requires the following:
- knowledge that we can acquire through education and experience,
- rational calculations with no mistakes,
- creativity,
- self-control, and
- anticipation.

Unfortunately, all of the features of the brain which are necessary to make good decisions can be compromised by watching pornography. Entrepreneurs take special care of their mind and they want to keep it in good condition whatever it takes. They sleep properly, exercise, and avoid stimulants. They often maintain a balanced diet or use vitamin and mineral supplements that help maintain high intellectual performance throughout the day. Businesspeople know that by engaging in appropriate activities and following good eating habits, they are able to optimally exploit the opportunities offered by the human mind. The myth that we only use 10% of our brains' capacity has permeated pop culture. Meanwhile, the truth is that we use 100% of our brains, as shown by simple MRI studies. Still, we can considerably improve the efficiency of our brains: remember better, concentrate more, process information faster, and solve more complex problems. It is also true that the brain, which accounts for approximately 3–5% of the body's weight, consumes about 20% of its resources, mainly oxygen and glucose. It is very important to keep your body in good shape and to provide it with the right amount of energy, vitamins, and minerals. Ejaculating too frequently and consuming the resources needed to rebuild semen reserves can diminish the means required for the efficient functioning of other organs, including the brain.

People who need brain efficiency in their day-to-day work are well aware that not only physical factors can affect its functioning. The brain becomes fatigued in the same way as the muscles do, so if we occupy it with non-essential matters, we will not have enough resources left to deal with vital things. What has a huge bearing on the human brain is the information we allow to enter it, and how and what we think about it. Successful people not only avoid distractions, but they also avoid unnecessary excitement that can sap their motivation or their mind. They also avoid negative thinking—that is, the kind of thinking which can produce a bad mood. Sadness, bitterness, and resentment may curb their creativity and general fitness. Successful people cannot afford the worries, fear, or depression that may arise from frequently masturbating and watching pornography. They cannot afford to have lower testosterone levels, which would limit their ability to take risks and to explore the unknown.

People who want to maximize their productivity often stay away from not only erotic content, negative information, and toxic people, but also from advertising, news, and journalism. Human attention is a precious commodity and many businesses are fighting for it. Often, the more attention these businesses attract, the more effectively they work. This mainly applies to what are commonly referred to as "advertising spaces"—such as the entertainment industry, television, social networks, banners, billboards, posters, and newspapers—but it also applies to pornography websites. Only viewership and website traffic ratings count for them. For us, our attention is much more valuable. The time that we devote to watching pornography, to checking updates on social networks, to browsing news about events that we have no influence on, is time wasted for us. After all, we can use this time to learn, develop ourselves, practice our favorite sport, earn money, or take another step towards the objectives we have set for ourselves. If we want to undertake a really important activity, after consuming entertainment based on fast information or strong stimuli, we may be ineffective or incapable. Perhaps it would be too radical to completely exclude entertainment from our life, because hobbies or sports put us into a good mood or develop valuable skills, and this is necessary for creative work. It is worth noting, however, that the majority of the information we are bombarded with provokes either a neutral or a negative reaction in us. It is not so much that this news draws our attention, but that it causes us to worry and think about it. It drains from us the life energy we need for action.

For successful people, what counts is the information that reaches them. When they work, nothing must impede their concentration. They can't afford to think about things that don't concern them. Mental energy is tremendously important to them. There is the well-known theory that every little unnecessary decision required throughout the day—what to eat or what to wear, for example—exhausts our intellectual capacity. That is why Barrack Obama, Mark Zuckerberg, and Steve Jobs famously shunned any choices about what to wear or what to eat for dinner. They avoided such trivial decisions like the plague because they knew that they could restrain their ability to make other, more important and valuable decisions. This method may seem drastic, but focusing on the highest aspirations required them to help themselves in every way they could.

Think about the extent to which dilemmas such as what to eat and what to wear absorb your attention and decision-making powers. They are not that absorbing, right? In fact, you might get the impression that these decisions have a minimal impact on your mental fatigue and efficiency throughout the day. You have probably not yet experienced a situation in which these minimal resources of intellect were necessary to make a more important decision even slightly better. Now think about how much of your attention and mental strength is taken up by sexual stimulation, especially pornography. Hundreds of times more, right? The brain becomes almost intoxicated by these strong stimuli. The decision of whether to watch pornography at all, which film to watch, which actors to choose, repeated several times in a short period of time, already torments the mind, let alone the strong engagement in what we are watching. If we perform such an energy-intensive activity at least once a day, where do we get the mental strength to function for the rest of the day?

4. WHAT IS ON OUR MINDS?

Great minds discuss ideas, average minds discus events, small minds discuss people.

- Eleanor Roosvelt

4.1. PRECIOUS NOVELTY

On the road to success, it is very important to take care of the mind and to critically approach the information and erotic content we are bombarded with. The reward mechanism for novelty is worth mentioning. It works by making us feel a little better when we're watching something fresh, visiting an unfamiliar place, or learning something new. When the reward system was being developed, this mechanism was intended to mobilize us to explore the terrain and to invent things that could facilitate our survival. Thanks to this same mechanism, we feel that we are satisfying our curiosity through reading a new article on a news website. This mechanism is also responsible for addiction to the Internet. Many people are unable to refrain from surfing the web. Involuntarily, they sit in front of their computer and click on the most eye-catching headlines and banners. It is this mechanism which causes us to spend so much time browsing the Internet. It is not true that websites are unnecessary in our lives, because through them we can communicate with our loved ones and can access important and valuable information. However, a lack of control over which news we access and which sources we find it from can be destructive. This side of the Internet makes us inquisitive and tempts us to peep into people's lives. Under the guise of entertainment, it engages us in matters that we would not normally engage in. This is when we lose the most of our precious energy. After a session in front of a computer spent on mindless surfing, reading posts from people we barely know, or watching pornography, we feel mentally drained.

When we browse the Internet, our brain releases small doses of dopamine, which encourage us to seek more new information. Another website opened is another novelty. As I mentioned, this mechanism is also responsible for maintaining arousal in pornography users. When the porno we are watching starts to bore us and doesn't turn us on enough, we move on to a new video and a new naked woman. This allows us to sustain the state of sexual excitement. Only when dopamine doses stop satisfying us do we get bored and we leave the computer. Then, mental exhaustion also appears.

After such online voyages, we have no desire for

anything new for a while. Because of the intensely exciting novelties which are literally at our fingertips, the brain stops responding to other, much more important novelties at some point. And yet this mechanism would push us to discover the unknown! It is this mechanism which makes us excited about trying new restaurants and meeting new acquaintances. It's sad that we often give up many colorful experiences in life just because we can see them on the computer screen.

The mechanism of rewarding us for novelty also becomes activated when we look for new ideas and try to come up with something innovative. When we set ourselves the goal of finding a new product, creating a new service, or designing an object or scheme, the brain begins to secrete small doses of dopamine which mobilize us to act and create new products. It's amazing that when we begin the creative process, the brain gives us such a large dose of natural energy. Our thinking sharpens instantly, facts are much easier to connect, and our capacity to remember becomes greater and clearer. We are only a few thoughts away from synthesizing a new idea. When a new idea crystallizes, the reward mechanism induces a feeling of happiness and satisfaction. At the very moment we discover something groundbreaking, when we come up with a business idea or craft a unique design, or when our creation meets with approval and demand, we experience a state of euphoria. Without this mechanism, it would be very tough to come up with a good idea. Unfortunately, this natural ease of creation will not be triggered when we deplete our potential with unnecessary information, trivialities, and pornography. Interestingly, dopamine—which we obtain during the creative process—is also addictive. This is one of the few addictions that positively influence people and society.

Does this sound implausible? Think about what drove such inventors as Leonardo da Vinci, Thomas Edison, Nikola Tesla, and Albert Einstein. These people created dozens, or even hundreds, of inventions. They constantly had new ideas, they discovered uncharted territory, and they even devoted their whole lives to this pursuit. If it hadn't been for their addiction to discovering new things, we may not be enjoying such prosperity today. These inventors differed from contemporary researchers in that they didn't have access to such a vast array of information. From the perspective of today's science, taking into account the access to resources that we enjoy today, it can be said that their discoveries came out of nowhere. They couldn't just open a web browser and look something up in a few minutes. They needed determination and unlimited patience. They studied books for hours, traveled to distant libraries, and had to remember most of the knowledge they read. Despite that, their discoveries were milestones in the progress of humanity.

Unfortunately, today we hear less and less about such astounding inventions as the telephone, the steam engine, or the theory of relativity. If you think about it, all of the new inventions around us are based on previous ideas. TV sets with larger screens, computers with faster and faster processors, smaller portable hard drives with more memory. Even modern electric cars using cutting-edge technology rely on ideas which were conceived years ago. We can say that there have been fewer and fewer discoveries and inventions that are important for humanity. Perhaps we don't find out about many inventions because they are unable to penetrate the public's consciousness. Perhaps new discoveries which could bankrupt existing businesses are kept secret. On the other hand, the global population is growing faster and faster, and we are not moving forward as fast as before. There are three times as many of us as there was in the 1950s. Despite living a more comfortable life, we work harder and longer. Perhaps there is less and less to discover, so progress has slowed down. Or perhaps it isn't so easy to notice new demand because all of our needs have already been met.

However, we still aren't able to save the environment, to eliminate hunger and poverty, to cease military operations, or to treat many diseases. It is very likely that most people have stopped seeking something truly new in the form of discoveries and inventions. Information and eroticization bombarding us from all sides has effectively lulled our natural tendency to pursue new goals and to venture into the unknown. In addition, a growing number of men have a reduced testosterone level, which is responsible for the determination to explore. I may be generalizing, but a lot of human potential is squandered in front of televisions and computers. Who knows, if people didn't spend so much time consuming unnecessary information, we might be travelling freely to other planets. Perhaps then we would be able to give up the non-renewable energy sources and would solve all our other problems once and for all?

4.2. IDEAS PRODUCE VALUE

Every enterprise, every business, every discovery—everything starts with an idea. There are many ways in which you can help yourself find new ideas. The potential of the human brain is uncharted. The important thing is not to limit this potential. You already know how unnecessary information and eroticization can sap your thought process. You need to be able to rely on your mind. You're probably thinking: "I can stop wasting my time on nonsense, stop watching pornography, but I still won't know where to get these ideas from." Ideas don't just fall out of the sky. I mentioned before that an idea is usually synthesized from the information you already possess. When you stop littering your head with unnecessary information and gain the desire to look for new ideas, you will start synthesizing them.

Specifically speaking, you will start reading industry news, taking a closer look at how the businesses around you operate, reading biographies of famous business people, and paying attention to people's needs and the markets around you. Almost every object in your surroundings is an element of some kind of business. Even if you are reading this book in a park, everything you see can be the spark of some new business. Every item you own is probably a product of a profitable company. Maybe what I'm writing seems banal to you, but look closely at an object or service within your view. Consider what the production process looked like, how much it cost to produce, what its retail price was, its wholesale price, or whether you'd need aggressive marketing to sell it. That's exactly how I practiced my ability to create new business ideas.

Very few innovative ideas become a hit on the market. It even turned out that many innovative ideas were so far ahead of their time that the markets hadn't developed demand for them yet. A lot more of the successful businesses thrive on conventional products and everyday services. Sometimes, it's enough to come up with a new packaging idea or a catchy name. If you already have a passion in life, then it will be easy for you to transform that into an idea. If you have been trained or are getting educated in a particular profession, then it will be easy for you to look for ideas in your field. Maybe you'll be able to find a niche market for a specialized product or service. Often, simple ideas—or those related to a seemingly saturated industry—do very well on the market, and thanks to people's enthusiasm and creativity they can expand and dominate. It is precisely these existing businesses that often become the inspiration for innovation and improvement.

There are plenty of sources of inspiration around you that can help you find an idea. The Internet, bookstores, and libraries are full of titles related to running a business. In fact, the best-selling books are business books. I recommend exploring available information about the basics of how a company operates, management, company finances, and the laws which regulate business. These are integral parts of any company doing business. Interestingly, you will need to acquire this knowledge sooner or later in your business venture. It may be that you are already working for some company, so it will be easy for you to put this knowledge into practice. You will be able to find out how your employer generates income, how high the costs are, and how profitable his or her business is. You may even discover ways to improve this company.

One interesting source of inspiration is motivational business books, which are available in abundance today. The ones which inspired me the most were the biographies of great authorities on business, such as Henry Ford and Benjamin Franklin, and the classics of the self-development genre, such as *Think and Grow Rich* by Napoleon Hill, as well as several other contemporary business titles which you can easily find recommendations for online. However, it is more important to gain specific knowledge in a given area and to try to put your ideas into practice. The book market is almost inexhaustible and you can infinitely explore knowledge which can be useful to you. It is important not to get stuck at the stage of motivating and educating yourself, but instead to focus on your ideas and on implementing them. I must admit that from time to time I go back to the same books to get motivated and to brush up on my knowledge. I do it very rarely, though, because I simply don't have time for it—I'm busy with my ideas almost non-stop.

4.3. MONEY DOESN'T GROW ON TREES (FIRST UNSUCCESSFUL BUSINESSES)

At some point in my life, I noticed that when I spend my time watching pornography, and then eventually recover from it, I miss out on some things. More and more often, I envied the success of young entrepreneurs who set up impressive businesses based on new technologies. The money that I had at my disposal did not allow me to make my dreams come true, so I wanted to have more and more of it. In addition, I experienced a growing number of the problems listed in the second chapter. Already suspecting—but not yet fully aware of—what havoc pornography and masturbation were wreaking in my body, I decided to limit them. This proved to be very tough. I was convinced that it would be impossible to completely give up the habit. I probably didn't want to lose one of the few pleasures in my life.

Shortly after I first decided to curtail pornography and masturbation, my mind began to cry out for some sort of occupation. I started to read more and renewed my friendships. I spent less and less time alone in my room. At that time, my friends recommended the books I mentioned above. I hadn't even finished reading them when my awakened imagination ordered me to act. I didn't have much capital, but I was determined to succeed. After all, every self-made man also started from scratch. I began to see all those high walls that had blocked my path tumble down. My parents didn't see it that way. They were paying for my education and they hoped I would spend every moment of my free time on my internship at a bank. They were disappointed with my frivolity. They thought that when I was alone in a room with a computer, I must have been doing something constructive. Unfortunately, they were wrong, and the last thing I needed was to be alone in front of the computer. Now, I know that it was best to admit to my weakness. I'm sure that my parents would have helped me, but at the time I didn't dare to confess the truth so I gradually dealt with my problem on my own. My family was not very wealthy. My studies were a burden for them, and now I was exposing them to higher costs. The awareness that I didn't have the support of my family weighed heavily on me. However—I do not know why—I naïvely believed that everything I embarked on would be successful.

My first business ideas were quite simple and didn't require a large financial outlay, but they gave me a lot of experience. The first one was a food stand. I thought of this idea before the summertime while I was in college. I had just turned 20 and it seemed to me that gastronomy wasn't a very challenging industry; after all, I could cook for myself from time to time. I decided to build a catering cart and to hire an employee to fry crêpes with peanut butter and maple syrup. The business was meant to be located at the lakeside summer resort near my hometown. It was supposed to be a seasonal business, generating income as I went out on a boat or lay face-up on the beach.

When the cart was still under construction, I started looking for an employee. I figured that everything had to be locked up airtight by the beginning of the season. I mean, any delay could cause a loss of income. I walked around town and talked to teenagers who I knew from school. These guys were hanging around with nothing to do. One of them, Jacob, immediately expressed a willingness to work. I hired him on the spot. He was kind of surprised when I showed up at his home with some equipment: a bottle of gas, a supply of flour, milk and filling, and I told him, "From now until we open, you're going to eat crêpes every day. You'll feed them to your family till you can cook them perfectly." His parents and younger sister looked at me like Indians must have looked at the first Europeans. Jacob was confused but he nodded timidly. I admit I was behaving strangely, but I considered this to be typical of business authorities.

My idea promised to be a hit and I was determined to see it through. Friends jokingly congratulated me on my intellect and asked me not to forget about them when I become a millionaire. I turned a deaf ear to their jokes... but they were right. My business didn't even last a week. The first setback was the sanitation inspection: they didn't authorize me because there was no running water or a refrigerator. When I got both of those connected, I discovered that there were practically no tourists in the area where my food stand was to operate. My vision of that place came from the days when regular folks went to nearby towns for vacation. In the meantime, budget airlines had appeared and people had begun to travel further than across their neighbor's field. Small towns along a murky lake weren't the attractions they once were. Although my cart had wheels, it stood in one place because of the requirement to have access to water and electricity. To top it all off, the weather was awful that summer, and the cart didn't have much in terms of rain protection.

Unfortunately, due to the limited funds I had for investment and the increasingly unstable situation on the market, I closed the business. I remember very well the stress I felt then. My head hurt and I just wished I could open my eyes and be somewhere else. I had invested all my savings into this venture, over $1,000 which I saved up over a few years of temporary jobs. There was still the problem of Jacob, because I had promised him a job. Almost on cue, though, he called me to say that his parents thought I was insane and forbade him to work for me. At least one problem had resolved itself. I definitely lacked people skills and the ability to cope with stress. I managed to sell some of the equipment at a small profit, which allowed me to get out of this business with only a small loss.

That same summer, I invested the rest of my money in T-shirts with typical designs. I thought it would be better to be a distributor and to scrap the issues with sanitation and employees. I was sure that this business would become the lifeline that would allow me to get back on track. After all, my design ideas were original and my friends liked them. I proudly distributed my products to souvenir stalls within a 20-mile radius. The shopkeepers I visited usually had somber faces, but agreed to accept the merchandise on credit. I set a price with them and suggested the profit margins. I didn't bat an eye at their total lack of enthusiasm. About 10 out of 100 T-shirts were sold that season, most of them to friends and family. The following season was even worse. Some of the owners of the stands went into another business and neither they nor my T-shirts were heard from ever again. I collected what was left and to this day I have spare T-shirts, which I give to friends as birthday presents.

That's how my first business ideas and experiences looked. What I liked most was my eagerness, excitement, and strength, which allowed me to enter into these ventures. I had to face some stress in the later stages, but the knowledge I gained from the experience was priceless. If I hadn't been paralyzed by the thought of losing money, I might have continued with these ideas. I couldn't control myself at all. It was a precious lesson for someone as inexperienced as I was then, though this could have been avoided. Running a company means constantly acquiring new information and making difficult decisions. Before you go into any business, you first need to do exhaustive market research—and above all, to be emotionally ready for this step. You can't invest money blindly, while naïvely believing that everything will go your way. You must have knowledge. It was only later that I learned about gastronomy, which I should have done before going into business. It is one of the more stable industries, which I couldn't convince myself of back then. It can't be run at minimum costs, though, and requires long-term commitment. I've also read about the textile industry: where and how to produce clothes, the prices for ready-made products from the import market, and the prices for locally sewn clothes. I've learned something about relationships with customers and suppliers, too. You shouldn't always leave merchandise with retailers on credit, as not everyone is honest. If the sellers are dishonest, they will only pay if they are dependent on subsequent deliveries. I remember how the people who prepared those T-shirts for me were astounded that I paid cash when picking up the goods. At that time, I had no idea what financial liquidity is or how to maintain it. I secretly thank myself for not taking out bank loans for these businesses or borrowing from suppliers. On the one hand, I may not have had much motivation for action (meaning, a knife to my throat), but on the other hand, I wasn't afraid to forfeit these ventures. Let's be honest: self-confidence, perseverance, and strength are necessary to run a business, but common sense is also needed. At that time, I had no common sense.

4.4. MORE INFORMATION MEANS MORE OPPORTUNITIES

After this memorable summer, I was feeling kind of low. It was difficult for me to recover from the bitterness of failure. Unfortunately, I did the worst thing possible; that is, I returned to pornography. This time I tried to limit playing with myself, but once more I stopped dealing with the emerging tension. I was again at risk of being alone in a room with my computer. However, thanks to my experiences in business, I began to apply myself more to learning. While I was still in college, I forced myself to find a job in which I could gain more experience and earn the means to set up possible new businesses. That's how I started working as an auditor in one of the Big 4 audit firms. This news really raised my parents' spirits. A lot of my friends and many famous entrepreneurs gained their first professional experience in the auditing industry. Everyone recommends working as an auditor at the start for those who don't know yet what they intend to do with their career but wish to learn business from the inside. Fortunately, the auditing departments in consulting companies are not as demanding of candidates as the other departments are. Bear in mind that during that time I behaved as if I lived in a fantasy world. I suddenly went from being a lazy malcontent to stubbornly wanting to become a smooth operator. I lacked basic experience and skills and I had no soft skills because of my social anxiety. I threw myself in at the deep end, but today I am grateful for it.

After my first business failure, my morale was not very high. Luckily, I tried to refrain from watching pornography, so I didn't suppress my natural talents like before. Though I was still shy, I was slowly beginning to feel better among people and I learned to give the impression of being composed. When I think back on who I was at that time, I definitely wouldn't trust myself with any responsibility, no way. The recruiter didn't know that I hadn't made a single smart move in the past few years. What's more, I had minimal knowledge from my university classes and practically no skills that could be useful in this position. On my résumé, I wrote "economics degree, not yet completed," and a few stories loosely based my work experience. I barely passed their pre-employment tests with the minimum score required, and I performed adequately at the interview. I answered the soft skills questions correctly, but answered the professional ones evasively or erroneously. Fortunately, the end of the fiscal year was approaching, so a lot of workers were needed to help audit financial statements, and they provided some introductory training before starting work. Since some candidates chose other job offers, there was a position for me. So I was hired as an assistant in the auditing department.

Then, my first serious job became a real drag. This may sound strange, but it turned out that I can't work. Just getting up in the morning and wearing a suit all day made me tired. This wasn't the main problem, because I was almost never late and my shirt was clean and ironed every day. The point is that I couldn't concentrate on intellectual work for more than 10 minutes. I couldn't focus on one task and see it through, because the habit of reaching for instantly available information and pleasure made me check my phone, social networks, and messages constantly. I had to turn off my phone and block some websites on my work computer. Additionally, most of the people working in the audit department were women. At that stage, I was only cutting back on pornography, and my brain often and effectively produced unwanted sexual associations. I couldn't get down to work because I was constantly undressing my colleagues in my mind. I associated professional small talk with flirtation, like in the beginning of a pornographic movie. When I caught on to this, I began to avoid unnecessary conversations with women and tried not to stare at them, not to look at their legs, butts, and busts.

This helped, but only partly. I always had to remind myself to check something in the receipts, to double-check everything I was doing, or that it was time for coffee or tea, and my work moved at a snail's pace. After surviving until lunchtime, dragging out and postponing essential tasks, I would soon notice that my mental performance was beginning to fail. As I returned to interrupted tasks, I often wouldn't remember where I had left off, and I sometimes couldn't even remember what it was I was doing. My mental capacities were so limited that I couldn't handle a few hours of work. My self-control turned out to be close to zero. You can probably guess how upset my bosses were with me when the work was on hold and I was constantly asking about something, often several times about the same thing.

My libido, confidence, and attitude were still laughable. I felt insecure almost all of the time. I had the persistent feeling that I was working ineptly and that I would soon be fired. I kept thinking that my days in this company were numbered. Twenty percent of my working time was allotted to learning about the client's company, about the mechanisms of their business, and the complexities in the account books, while eighty percent of the time was for preparing audit documentation. As you may imagine, my employers were mostly interested in the documentation. I was hopeless with the paperwork, but I managed somehow to learn the client's business. All in all, from the point of view of my employer's needs, I was superfluous. Luckily, I was able to get along with people there, and that was the only thing that allowed me to keep my job. Perhaps because of staff shortages, or perhaps out of pity, I was allowed to stay and finish out my contract.

Thanks to that little episode in the auditing industry, I had my first taste of real business. Do you know how it feels to suddenly learn everything about someone else's company? Such information is confidential, but that doesn't change the fact that it is knowledge you have and can use. During an audit, everything is investigated: what the prices are, who pays the invoices, who the supplier is, how much the wholesale goods cost, who owes money to whom, how the receivables flow in, how much people earn, who is evading taxes, and how they do it. In those six months, I learned how telecommunications, media, advertising, construction, and wholesale companies operate. I found out how trade functions in operational and financial terms. I reviewed inventories in manufacturing and distribution companies. I saw how stock management and logistics look. I discovered how much an international star receives for appearing in a commercial and I learned how much it costs to order 10,000 of the latest smartphones wholesale. It was a goldmine of information. I learned how existing businesses function, and that was much better than the theory I studied at college. I understood then why I had so little interest in studying. I just didn't have the opportunity to see how the theory translates into practice. I learned a great deal thanks to my job in the auditing firm, and all that paperwork has helped me to become more precise and to focus on tasks better, despite the fact that a long time had passed before I learned to do it diligently.

I also learned something very important about myself: I learned that I am not suited to working in a corporation. I missed the constant learning and decision-making which I experienced when I was running a business. When working on our own projects, we acquire knowledge in many areas—not only in accounting—and we constantly take decisions and risks. We risk our resources and time. Initially, this comes with stress, which we must learn to master and even to completely eliminate. In the corporate environment, there was also stress—but a different kind of stress. It came from being afraid of my boss's wrath and of losing my job. That's not the point, though. Handling the risk was the most valuable experience for me and that's what I wanted to do with my life. I wanted to take risks—specifically, to learn about and minimize them thanks to my knowledge, and only then to take them. The limited opportunities to learn new things and the lack of creativity in auditing work did not encourage me to continue working in the industry any longer.

When I left my job in auditing, I had already gained some valuable experience, and I knew that real, lasting business would not just appear at the snap of my fingers. For that, you need the right combination of knowledge, patience, creativity, capital, and determination. With this realization, I was ready to carry on searching for ideas. I became a realist when looking at the business world. My unhealthy, blind enthusiasm had vanished. Some humility and determination to learn more entered the picture. I knew that I needed to look for inspiration and know-how. I knew that I couldn't bite off more than I could chew. I also knew that it's not easy to invest the last of your remaining funds. It's better to have more capital and to invest a fraction of it—it's easier to control your emotions then. After my experience in the auditing department, I decided that I needed to look for a job that is even more closely linked with business. I chose investment banking. I did some research on the industry and I started to develop the necessary skills. Investment banking is an area for the brightest people who are colloquially called "pistols" in this line of business. They can count quickly and quickly connect the dots; they are confident, determined, and reliable. Unfortunately, I was still a mediocre student with no relevant experience and with a weakness for pornography, so I didn't find a job right away. It took me a long time before I adopted the right attitude. While finishing my degree and unsuccessfully going to job interviews, I was looking for other sources of income in the meantime.

4.5. THE FIRST SUCCESSFUL BUSINESS

My ideas were focused on the internet. I alternated watching pornography and setting up short-sighted, fly-by-night businesses. There are many ideas on the Internet about how to earn money. Online business usually goes well and the market—with the right approach—is receptive. First, I tried offering services: designing simple websites, logos, and banners, and developing web positioning. I mastered these skills with ease, but the competition was too intense for me to treat this as a serious occupation. It demanded a lot of time and the will to fight for projects, and my poor motivation was not up to such a task.

Then I moved on to something like dropshipping. I sourced a commodity from a country where it was cheaper to buy and sold it in another country where it cost more or was not available at all. Most often these were mobile phones and small electronic devices from China. Usually, I did not actually have the product, and when I made a sale I ordered it from the cheaper source and sent it to the buyer. Sometimes I bought goods from a supplier that were sent directly to the address of the buyer. I wouldn't recommend doing this because it may conflict with the local laws. Also, there were often complications such as delays in delivery, defective products that I hadn't checked being delivered, and problems with complaints. These experiences allowed me to understand that wheeler-dealer businesses typically don't have great prospects.

It was only later that I switched to online sales of a commodity I actually owned. I come from a small town where there were no shopping malls. In order to not look like a farmer I had to buy clothes online, and since I was not very wealthy I only bought things on sale. Living in the larger city where I was studying, I had access to large shopping malls and outlets, so I could sell clothes online to people living in rural areas. I went shopping on sale days and later posted the goods on auction websites at attractive prices. I soon noticed which items were selling faster and which weren't selling. The fastest-selling items were limited-edition shoes, which the outlets were full of and which collectors fought fiercely for. To my surprise, this developed into a business which allowed me to earn decent money. My rented room looked comical: it was filled with boxes of shoes and there was a pile of designer clothes on top of those boxes. I basically lived in a warehouse. I often slept with my head resting on a box of shoes. My friends had a good laugh when they saw the conditions I was living in. I also spread the word at my university that I had some clothes and shoes to sell, so from time to time someone came and bought what caught their eye. Turnover was reasonably fast, and the profit margins were satisfactory. My experience in auditing helped me in this business, more specifically, it helped me to watch my cash flow, manage my inventory, and keep the books, so that I could track the profitability of my business and keep looking for improvements in various areas.

After some time, competition appeared and a price war ensued. In addition, my suppliers' prices were slowly rising, so the business became less and less profitable. I had to choose either to dedicate myself to this entirely (expand my business, look for new suppliers, rent a warehouse, or set up a real online store) or give up. My limited motivation and lack of self-control effectively inhibited me from getting more involved and taking such a risk. I was aware that growing the business would mean a lot more work. I was also afraid of the competition, as I had limited capital. In addition, I still felt the bitterness of my failed summer business. I gave up selling clothes and slowly sold the rest of my stock. I allowed myself to finish college and I continued looking for employment in investment banking.

That was a very good time for me. I underwent a major change: from an antisocial freak to a slightly shy entrepreneur. I was slowly beginning to notice the pernicious influence of pornography and masturbation, so I managed to limit them. After that year, my mind recovered somewhat: my thoughts were clearer, my memory was better, and my deductions were sharper. I was gaining more and more experience and my actions were becoming more effective. My appetite for success grew, and larger and larger figures appeared in my imagination. I also had more and more interesting ideas.

5. I'M THE CAPTAIN NOW

*Most powerful is he who has himself
in his own power.*

- Seneca

5.1. INTANGIBLE ASSETS

I don't want to start this chapter sounding like a motivational speaker or a salesperson from an MLM scheme,[51] but first I must present you with a few clichés. You've probably already heard them, but it's good to remind ourselves of them from time to time. However, in order not to sound too banal, I will present some information and research that may change your perception of what is necessary to achieve a desired goal. I will also tell you how I turned my weaknesses into strengths.

It is said that we are the architects of our own future, that it is entirely up to us how much we prosper in life. Few people would say that we have no influence on our own destiny. Nowadays, we can affect almost every aspect of our lives. We can avoid diseases, have bodies like Greek statues, fill our heads with knowledge, and improve our memory and deductive reasoning. We can build capital, plan huge projects, and we can implement them. We can strive for lofty goals as well as smaller ones. We can endeavor to create a happy life for ourselves and to make our loved ones happy. Everything depends on what we want to do with our life. All of our satisfaction in life can stem from the fulfillment of our mission and the path we take. Often, travelling that path is a source of happiness in itself. It is important to be mindful of being on the road and moving forward along it. However, it is easy to get lost or to stray from your path in life, to become enticed by something lying on the side of the road, and to stay in one spot.

Unfortunately, many things in life give us an illusory feeling of happiness, which lasts but a moment and can distract us from what's more important. These include alcohol, drugs, pornography, gluttony, and excessive entertainment. It is imperative not to deviate from the path and not to quash our natural happiness. Unnatural stimuli and good times that provide temporary, illusory joy simultaneously deprive us of the joys of ordinary life. The

---

[51] Multi-Level Marketing – typically, personal sales and building vertical sales structures which demand the power of persuasion

qualities we have that deliver true happiness can easily be destroyed today. This results in addiction and in impaired living. We must not allow these stimuli to control us. We must not let a false, momentary joy manipulate us. We must not subordinate our life to artificial stimulation. We must remember that our bodies, that we ourselves, are able to achieve happiness and limitless joy, and that all half-measures will distance us from this goal.

People who doggedly pursue their goals and do not depart from life's path are well-motivated. Well-motivated people usually do not drink, do not smoke, do not party too much; they win medals at the Olympics, drop dozens of pounds in a few months, get into the best universities, and accumulate great wealth. The same people also foster happy families, help the poor, care for the environment, and fight injustice, and they deny themselves fleeting pleasures in order to achieve all this. Motivation seems to be something magical, something that apparently exists somewhere, but which only a few of us have managed to master. Those who haven't experienced motivation are often obese, addicted, ill-educated, or poor. Or maybe the motivated people just know more than others?

Motivation is not only a hormonal mechanism in the brain which is responsible for dopamine and the reward system, but it's also the ability to put big, long-term goals and satisfaction before short-term pleasures and instant gratification. In other words, motivation is also prioritization. It often happens that if we give up doing something pleasant now, we automatically get closer to a distant but much more enjoyable goal, so it's vital to be aware of this. The simplest example of prioritization is abandoning an unhealthy diet and poor eating habits, which in the long run translates into a slim figure and good health. Another example is learning, thanks to which we will gain a valuable education, and thus better earnings in the future.

There are plenty of examples of good prioritization. If I had been aware of the effects of prioritization throughout my life, I probably would have gone to a lot fewer parties, not used any drugs, studied a lot more, and spent less time with those friends who I've since lost touch with. I certainly would have avoided masturbation and steered clear of pornography, which also caused me to lose sight of my priorities.

Everyone wants a long, happy and affluent life, but hardly anyone can deny themselves little pleasures in order to achieve it. Is motivation enough when, for example, we are on a diet and our stomach is growling? Is motivation enough when our eyes ache from reading and we want to sleep, but we still have loads of material to revise for the exam? That's when willpower comes in handy. Thanks to willpower, we can overcome procrastination and quit cigarettes and other addictions. Thanks to willpower, we say no to excessive eating or pornography. Willpower guarantees that motivation can be brought to fruition. However, it will be much easier if, instead of willpower, we talk about self-control. In fact, the main factor which influences how we live, what we achieve, and where we are heading is self-control. The way our life plays out depends on conscious decisions about what the body should do at any moment. It is thanks to self-control that we can stay on our chosen path in life.

When we are on a diet and we feel like eating sweets, we decide whether we eventually reach for them. Will we respond to the signal from the stomach, which suggests that if we don't eat a few hundred more calories we will die? After all, we know perfectly well that our body has already received the necessary minimum calories, water, vitamins, and minerals to function efficiently and for a long time. When we are running in a race for a medal, and our body says that it can no longer run and we feel pain in every muscle, will we leave the race? We know perfectly well that after reaching the finish line we will rest and our body will quickly recover. The same notion applies to sexual tension, which means that at any given moment it seems to us that only by yielding to this desire can we find relief. But it really is enough to force ourselves to do something different, to change our surroundings and occupy our mind with something else in order to make that tension go away. Often, the signals that the body sends are wrong, and self-control consists of identifying these misleading signals.

In previous chapters, I explained how significantly the reward system can impact our behavior and how archaic this mechanism is. This system was formed when food was very difficult to find, when breeding offspring required a lot of effort and beating the competition, when new things were hardly ever encountered, and when the overall probability of survival in those conditions was much lower than at present. Today, we do not have to worry about anything. Most countries of the world provide their citizens a guarantee of survival at the very least. The reward system that once was necessary for us to survive is now the source of temporary pleasure, and often ruin. Through effortless stimulation of the reward system, people develop addictions, pig out without restraint, and spend a large part of their lives watching pornography. It is almost unethical the way many businesses profit from the weaknesses of the human body. That is why in our times the extent to which we control our bodies is so important. That's why it's so important to motivate yourself to achieve long-term goals and give yourself a reason for good self-control.

I called this subsection "intangible assets" because we ourselves are such assets, and more precisely, any skill that we master through practice is such an asset. As far as finances go, the term "intangible assets" usually signifies intellectual value such as computer programs, design patterns, important contracts, or licenses. It's difficult to quantify the value of a business manager or qualified employees and add it to the company's assets, but this value largely determines the attractiveness of the business for investors. It's true that an interesting idea and a reliable business model may be of interest to financiers, but the decision to finance is largely dependent on the assessment of the person behind this business. Motivation and high self-control are the most important intangible assets that we can develop and cultivate, because thanks to them we will be able to constantly evolve and grow our value.

5.2. RESEARCH ON SELF-CONTROL

You have to wonder what is more important for success in life: self-control or intelligence? Both of these features are probably important. At the same time, researchers indicate that one's level of self-control and one's level of intelligence do not correlate with each other. You can be intelligent and not control yourself, and vice versa. However, people with more self-control are more likely to achieve success because they develop the necessary skills very easily. It is comforting to know that we can all practice our self-control, expand our knowledge, and acquire new abilities. It's worth noting that people of above-average intelligence often do not find happiness in life, and are even more likely to be depressed, while people with more self-control find happiness in life more readily. Self-control helps them to achieve motivation, while priorities—that is, appropriate motivation—helps to reinforce self-control.

There is no doubt that the ability to relinquish temporary pleasures for the sake of a larger, delayed pleasure requires self-control. It can be assumed that the experience of self-control from previous years is also the foundation for the skill of self-control later in life. People who control themselves for a longer period of time use less energy for self-control. Similarly, a soccer player who plays in many games will more easily physically endure an entire game than a player who plays less often. A trained brain consumes less energy, so it metabolizes less glucose. A brain with better self-control does this more economically.

What is self-control, exactly? Is it a practiced skill,

acquired experience, or perhaps inner strength? Roy F. Baumeister conducted a study on self-control.[52] He tried to answer the question, "What is self-control?" He wondered if self-control was a limited resource, i.e., whether our self-control will eventually run out if we are exposed to incentives that tempt us for a long time. Baumeister claims that self-control is like a muscle which, when used for too long, needs to rest in order to regain energy. In addition, this muscle can be trained to become even more powerful. To verify this theory, Baumeister conducted a series of experiments. In one of them, a group of subjects was subjected to two successive situations requiring self-control. The study was to show whether the self-control used in the first situation reduces the self-control in the next independent situation. Additionally, it was designed to answer the question of what self-control actually is:

• if it's a skill, then the first situation will positively affect the second one;
• if it's experience or knowledge, then the first situation will not affect the second one; and
• if it's an internal, exhaustible energy supply, then the first situation will negatively affect the second one.

The subjects were divided into two groups. Each participant was separately introduced to a room filled with the smell of freshly baked cookies, with two kinds of food placed inside: chocolate treats and radishes. The first group could eat whatever they wanted, while the second group could only eat radishes, abstaining from eating the desserts. In the second part of the experiment, both groups were asked to solve a puzzle that could not be solved. The time they spent before giving up the task was measured. In this way, the effect that the first situation had had on the subjects' perseverance and self-control was studied. It turned out that people from the first group—who didn't

---

[52] Baumeister RF, Bratslavsky E, Muraven M, Tice DM (1998): *Ego depletion: is the active self a limited resource?*

need to show self-control during the first part—tried to solve the puzzle for an average of 19 minutes, while the second group—who had to refrain from eating the treats—worked on the puzzle for an average of 8 minutes. The study showed that self-control is a resource that can run out. It also supported the hypothesis that self-control is neither an acquired skill nor knowledge gained. Apparently, resisting the temptation had come at a price, in the form of a reduction in self-control.

In the next study, students were asked to record a self-promoting video which would be presented to other students later on. Some of the respondents were asked to introduce themselves naturally, while the others were asked to do it in such a way as to give the impression of being well-liked and competent. In the next stage, the respondents watched a feature film—but before the screening, they were asked not to show any emotions. It turned out that those who had previously prepared the more demanding presentation about themselves experienced more difficulty not displaying emotions. These studies show quite clearly that the ability of self-control is limited.

According to Baumeister, the self-control muscle regenerates primarily at night, while we sleep. In his opinion, a person who is rested and who had a good night's sleep resists temptation more easily. Strong self-control contributes to controlling one's impulses[53] and to overcoming one's urges, which is necessary in goal-oriented activities. Self-control also plays a large role in the work environment, where we are subjected to distractions. Thanks to self-control, we are able to focus our attention on

---

[53] Malte Friese, Wilhelm Hofmann (2009): *Control me or I will control you: Impulses, trait self-control, and the guidance of behaviour.*

the task despite distracting circumstances.[54] In business, self-control is an invaluable feature. All activities, investments, and negotiations require a cool head. You can't give in to emotions and impulses. All activities must be based on a calm, objective assessment of the situation. Furthermore, self-control aids in accomplishing long-term goals. Thanks to that, we don't resign from gratification which is delayed and we don't change our minds while carrying out a long-term strategy, such as an investment strategy.

5.3. DEVELOPMENT OF SELF-CONTROL

Surely you must remember the moments when you lacked self-control. Many of us have experienced situations in which we abandoned an important goal: for example, we gave up studying for an important test, we reached for yet another piece of candy, or went back to pornography despite the resolution to stop. Many of us can remember moments when we lost our head: for example, panicking in a difficult situation, getting stressed out during an interview, or buying something we didn't need because of a pushy salesperson. When we recall these usually unpleasant situations, we may come to the conclusion that we are weak, that we lack willpower, and that we will suffer the consequences for the rest of our lives. Nothing could be further from the truth.

Researchers have shown that it's possible to boost one's

---

[54] Klaus-Helmut Schmidt, Marlen Hupke, Stefan Diestel (2012): *Does dispositional capacity for self-control attenuate the relation between self-control demands at work and indicators of job strain?*

self-control.[55] Regular exercises can considerably improve self-control and can enhance our resistance to the exhaustion of self-control, the same way that exercising your muscles will increase their mass and efficiency. One of the first studies on the subject, conducted by Muraven, Baumeister, and Tice in 1999,[56] suggested that the strength of self-control increases under the influence of exercise. First, participants were given a task to deplete their resources of self-control.[57] Then they were asked to perform one of three exercises for two weeks, which were meant to contribute to the growth of self-control: posture correction, nutrition control, or mood improvement. After two weeks, the participants were again tested for depletion of self-control resources. There was a general increase in self-control among the people performing exercises compared to the control group, who didn't perform any exercises. This experience suggested that exercise may improve self-control, but it should be remembered that this increase was not absolute, but only relative to the control group. In addition, only the exercise of maintaining correct posture led to significant gains.

---

[55] Roy F. Baumeister, Matthew Gailliot, C. Nathan DeWall, Megan Oaten (2006): *Self-Regulation and Personality: How Interventions Increase Regulatory Success, and How DepletionModerates the Effects of Traits on Behavior.*

[56] Muraven M, Baumeister RF, Tice DM (1999): *Longitudinal improvement of self-regulation through practice: building self-control strength through repeated exercise.*

[57] In a standard test examining the depletion of self-control resources, the subject performs a task that requires physical or mental exertion for as long as possible. He or she does this twice, and the time taken to do each of these tasks is measured. Between attempts, he or she gets another task that requires powerful self-control. In this case, the timed task was to keep a fist clenched around a handgrip, and the task requiring self-control was to suppress a thought, specifically, "Don't think about a white bear."

In another study, Oaten and Cheng more clearly demonstrated the relationship between self-control exercises and self-control resources.[58] They persuaded the participants to start a two-month physical training program. Each participant received an exercise program developed by gym employees, which included weight lifting, endurance exercises, and aerobic exercises. It was assumed that the exercises requiring increased self-control would positively affect the overall self-control of the participants. Before and after the exercises, the subjects underwent tests for self-control depletion. In the tests before the start of training, the participants demonstrated some level of exhaustion, which significantly decreased after 2 months of exercise. Interestingly, participation in the training programs brought additional benefits in other areas which require self-control. Participants of the study undergoing the training program indicated that they rarely drank alcohol, cut back on smoking, drank less coffee, ate less unhealthy food, and chose more healthy dishes. They also limited their television viewing and spent more time studying. They even pointed out things such as washing the dishes after a meal instead of leaving dirty dishes in the sink. It's easy to explain the relationship between regular exercise and improvements in diet, but it's difficult to link physical exercise and, for example, an increased devotion to studying in any way. All of this, however, suggests that the period of exercise—which required increased self-control—had a positive effect on self-control in all other areas of life. Currently, when prestigious companies are hiring, they often take into account whether the candidate belonged to a sports team at university or are committed to practicing any sports. The rigorous workouts can be assumed to have effectively trained the potential employee's self-control, which promises that they will be highly productive at work.

---

[58] Oaten M, Cheng K. (2006): *Longitudinal gains in self-regulation from regular physical exercise*.

Oaten and Cheng, in another study,[59] focused on something that proves to be the most costly consequence of an absence of self-control: they checked how personal finance management training affects one's overall self-control. Participants of the study underwent a four-month program of expenditure monitoring, before which each of them consulted with an adviser and received a money management plan. As a consequence of the study, the participants began to deal with money much better. None of the respondents increased their income thanks to the exercises, but the average savings rate increased from 8% to 38%. The research certainly brought good results in the form of developing personal finance management skills, which the participants were very happy with. But there was an improvement in areas other than finances as well. The respondents showed better self-control in the laboratory self-control test; they reduced alcohol, cigarette, and coffee intake; they better controlled their emotions, began to eat more healthily, and did better with their housework; and they began to cultivate better study habits.[60] One might suspect that putting aside money would encourage them to buy cheaper, less healthy food, but the habit of financial self-control also led to an interest in the quality of food. To sum up, in this case the exercise of self-control also improved willpower in other aspects of life.

The results of these studies unambiguously prove that self-control exercises bring results. However, it should be noted that these studies usually have relative effects, not absolute ones. Mark Muraven resolved to find out whether short-term acts of self-control affect better self-control

---

[59] M. Oaten, K. Cheng (2007): *Improvements in self-control from financial monitoring.* "Journal of Economic Psychology."

[60] Ibid.

when quitting smoking.[61] He hypothesized that a short, two-week period of self-control exercises would help you quit smoking more successfully. The researcher selected 122 volunteers who smoked at least 10 cigarettes throughout the day and who wanted to quit. For some, it was not their first attempt at quitting. The participants of the study were informed that if they performed the particular exercises conscientiously, they would quit smoking more effectively. Half of the respondents received tasks that required self-control, i.e., avoiding sweets or the handgrip exercises, and the other half—which also served as the control group—received tasks that only seemingly demanded self-control, i.e., solving very simple math problems or writing a journal. The subjects who performed tasks that did not require self-control were also convinced that they were exercising self-control. After the exercise program, the respondents proceeded to the main task: to stop smoking cigarettes. The results of the study were quite explicit. The respondents broke their resolution and lit up their first cigarette after, on average:

- 7.4 days for those solving simple mathematical tasks (the control group);
- 6.9 days for those writing a journal (the control group);
- 12.1 days for those avoiding sweets (participants exercising self-control); and
- 12.3 days for those clenching their fists (participants exercising self-control).

This means that exercises requiring self-control significantly increased the average time of abstinence from smoking. A month after quitting, only 12% of the participants in the control group remained abstinent, while 27% of the participants actually exercising self-control still had not lit up a cigarette. This experiment allows us to assert that the degree of effort we make during self-control

---

[61] Mark Muraven (2010): *Practicing Self-Control Lowers the Risk of Smoking Lapse*.

exercise is important. The effort which required a lot of self-control increased the time of abstinence, while the effort which didn't require much self-control did not produce such effects. It can also be concluded that the results didn't arise from the belief that the exercise would help, or from paying attention to self-control, but only from actual self-control training.

5.4. WEAKNESS AS AN ADVANTAGE

These experiments prove that general self-control can be practiced thanks to regular acts of self-control. This is very good news in the world of medicine. Many diseases result from an impairment of self-control skills. It seems that by strengthening one's self-control, one can treat addiction to alcohol, drugs, food, and cigarettes. This is very convenient because the exercise of self-control is cheaper than pharmacological or surgical treatments. Admittedly, self-control therapy is not as effective as the traditional methods, but it is certainly less invasive to the body. By boosting the skill of self-control, we can get rid of many bad habits, and at the same time have a positive impact on other aspects of our lives.

It's funny that the more bad habits we have, the better we can practice self-control by getting rid of them. From the studies mentioned above, it follows that by undertaking small acts of self-control, we can prepare for large ones. With more reserves of self-control, these large self-control acts become small ones. When we go on a diet and monitor our nutrition, we increase our amount of total self-control, which further allows us to quit cigarettes and pornography, for example. If we practice self-control with ever-greater acts of self-control, we will be able to control ourselves enough to systematically devote time to studying hard and perfecting our skills. What's more, these studies advocate the theory that the muscle of self-control is responsible for many areas in which self-control is essential. It can be concluded that if we give up a very heavy addiction, we will be able to—for example—study under very stressful circumstances, we'll become resistant to distractions, we'll be able to focus much longer on a task, and we'll increase our willpower in order to accomplish our objectives.

    Doesn't the title *Quit Porn and Get Rich* take on a much deeper meaning now? All those who regularly watch porn know how difficult it is to quit this addiction. Some online forums[62] have organized into support groups for those who are trying to recover from this compulsive habit. The forum members' boastful comments about the number of days they held out without masturbating to pornography are mixed with the confessions and regrets of others who couldn't endure and broke their resolutions. Still others claim that it is impossible to completely free yourself from pornography and masturbation. In the jargon of people visiting such forums, the term PMO (porn, masturbation, orgasm) is what this addiction is called. Yet, in my opinion, this abbreviation may anesthetize us to the truth and may downplay the problem. When using such acronyms, we can forget that we are dealing with a disorder that complicates our lives. Watching strangers have sex on-screen is a perversion, and the organ that was created for reproduction is not meant to be used for solitary games. Getting rid of this perpetually absorbing habit is undeniably tough, but possible. It doesn't require a ban on watching pornography so much as control over your thoughts and avoiding any stimuli that can cause you to feel the temptation. The process of breaking free of addiction doesn't forgive moments of weakness. Breaking the habit of watching pornography and masturbating requires outstanding self-control skills in every situation.

    1. We need to control every aspect of our lives in order to steer clear of the impulses and situations that

---

[62] https://www.reddit.com/r/NoFap

trigger the desire to watch pornography and masturbate.
2. We must avoid moments of weakness when our self-control is exhausted or prone to be easily exhausted.
3. We must be able to control ourselves when temptation appears.

There is probably no scale for assessing the intensity of tensions caused by particular addictions, but the tension caused by the need to watch pornography and masturbate seems to be one of the strongest. In addition, the mind often becomes an enemy to our resolutions, because under the influence of urges it quickly trivializes any resolution and suggests that giving in will not cause any great harm. Only after succumbing to the urge do doubt, sadness, and guilt come. So everything depends on how strong our self-control is. If someone is unable to control himself enough to cut pornography and masturbation out of his life, he can start with a smaller act of self-control. This way, he will train the muscle of self-control to cope with this or another addiction. It may be a good idea to start with diet and regular exercise. If, after a few weeks, you effortlessly avoid junk food and don't find yourself skipping the workouts, you'll be able to move on to more demanding resolutions, such as quitting smoking or studying regularly. As soon as you feel that you control other aspects of your life more and more easily, you can proceed to giving up pornography and masturbation. If you manage to tackle your greatest weaknesses, then you'll be able to control yourself in your quest for infinitely higher goals. This is just an example of how to train the muscle of self-control and how much you can benefit from it, by abandoning a habit and fulfilling your dreams, for example.

    There are certainly many aspects of your life that you can control and that can help you train your self-control muscle. Always keep in mind how harmful artificial stimuli are to you, especially pornography and masturbation. Remember that pornography, pornographic thoughts, and masturbation can do the following:

- impoverish your thinking,
- disrupt your attention,
- cloud your memory,
- weaken your counting skills and short-term memory,
- deprive you of other activities,
- lead to bad moods and depression,
- cause laziness and procrastination,
- skew your perception of relationships with women,
- cause physical weakness,
- lower your testosterone levels,
- make you shy,
- result in anxiety,
- erode your confidence, and
- consume your valuable time and energy.

With increased self-control and an awareness of the damage resulting from giving in, it will be much easier to avoid pornography and masturbation. After discontinuing pornography and masturbation:
- your mind will become more efficient,
- your testosterone level will rise,
- you will gain the strength to discover and venture into the unknown,
- your relationships with others will improve,
- your fear and anxiety will disappear,
- your self-confidence will rise, and
- your life will become more satisfying and joyful.

Think about how your muscle of self-control will strengthen if you succeed in permanently stopping pornography. The situation changes significantly if we treat this habit not as our weakness, but as a tool for training self-control necessary to achieve life goals and happiness. The advantage of abandoning pornography will be twofold: you will regain your natural strength and drive and firm up the muscle of self-control.

Perhaps it isn't just watching porn that is your weakness and you still need strong self-control to abandon other habits. Rejecting pornography and masturbation will surely give you strength. However, more self-control will also be handy for many other very important projects. This book is equally devoted to abandoning pornography (Quit Porn) and to achieving happiness in life (Get Rich). The power of self-control and of the natural energy suppressed by pornography is what's required to attain happiness and to realize your innermost dreams. My desire was to have a stable life, to start a family, and to provide myself with enough resources to not have to worry about financial matters. It was only when I started moving away from pornography and masturbation that I felt a strong desire and the incentive to achieve those inner dreams. Without it, it was difficult for me to overcome my laziness, lack of self-confidence, and fear, the time I had lost, and everything else connected with wasting my life on this devastating habit. And thanks to the fact that I got rid of it forever, I've gained the strength necessary to achieve my most ambitious goals. By conquering my weakness, I gave myself a real chance of fulfilling those ambitions. Also, because I was lucky enough to experience the wonderful results of this decision, I can describe my story, the entire path that I followed, and all of the challenges that I took on thanks to the internal strength which I renewed and reinforced. I returned to my true path in life and today I can talk about the aspects of life that would have been difficult for me to triumph over without a lot of self-control and the natural drive of the body.

5.5. QUITTING PORN

In recent times, Baumeister's theories have been contested, but I don't think these objections are justified. I strongly recommend that you read Dr. Roy Baumeister's book, *Willpower: Rediscovering the Greatest Human Strength*, as a supplement to this publication. I've experienced many situations in my life that required constant self-control. All of the interviews during which I had to pretend to be an ideal employee, and the negotiations during which I had to create the impression that I had a strong negotiating position, required incredible self-control from me. In life, you often need to keep a poker face, and sometimes even acting skills are demanded. When closing a strategic sale, negotiating an important deal, or finding a new investor, any behavior that raises doubt can bring about failure. The interviewers were watching closely to determine whether I was well-mannered, whether I felt confident with my qualifications, or whether I had the right approach to tasks. The conversations often lasted all day and with each subsequent task I found it harder and harder to maintain self-control. After such conversations, I usually felt completely drained of my self-control and I couldn't even pretend in front of my friends that the interview went well. A lot of large corporations and consulting companies deliberately set up their hiring process this way in order to test the candidate under the most extreme conditions, that is, when their self-control has already been exhausted.

I am reminded of my interview at the transaction advisory department of another Big 4 consulting company. The interview dragged on all day. It consisted of several stages, including a presentation in front of a group of managers, interviews with the HR department, filling out tests, and presenting the results. The last stage was a one-on-one interview with a manager from the department in question. None of the tasks required too much intellectual effort, yet my ideal employee attitude weakened by the hour. I confess that I couldn't control myself by the last stage of this ordeal. I completely lost control and started talking about all of my doubts and weaknesses in the hope that the interviewer would appreciate my honesty. As you might have imagined, I didn't get the job.

The same thing happened during the interview process for the consulting department of one of the famous Big 3 management consulting companies. In this case, the interview took almost an entire day. It began with difficult tests, followed by three interviews: with a woman from HR, a manager, and the director. Between the written test and the interview, they gave me some questions, most of which were difficult cases to be solved. In such situations, if you don't know how to solve the task, you have to improvise and pretend to be making on your way toward finding the solution. Unfortunately, by the second interview I couldn't pretend I even wanted to solve these tasks at all. I didn't get the job that time, either. All of this prompted me to consider what kind of man I needed to become so that in the future I wouldn't have problems obtaining my dream job, and to consider which personalities do better in the business world. In addition to the knowledge and experience that I had to have, it was necessary to practice self-control and to maintain good habits and attitudes.

Take, for example, Elon Musk and what he did in his youth.[63] He planned on moving to the US, but he wasn't sure what his future life would look like there. To see if he could survive on $30 a month—in case he failed to earn more money—he decided to try to live for a month on one dollar a day. He succeeded without too much trouble, which assured him that he didn't need a high salary to survive, a fact which allowed him to achieve much higher goals. According to him, he mainly ate sausages, oranges, and pasta, which he bought in bulk at low prices. This example shows how strong his self-control was in the early stages of his career. This has undoubtedly contributed to his success.

I painfully experienced the deficits in my self-control when I was working at the auditing firm (I couldn't focus on my work). Fortunately, the interviewers weren't so

---

[63] Rochard Felloni, "Business Insider" (2015): *Elon Musk explains why living off a dollar a day as a teenager convinced him he could do anything he wanted with his life*.

demanding at that time. After another round of about ten job interviews for consulting companies, I recognized that something was wrong with my body. I was too anxious and was perpetually insecure. I would become overwhelmed by fear suddenly and without reason. I couldn't assume a masculine, firm posture. I hesitated for too long and I couldn't make good decisions. Even when I knew the answer to the interviewers' questions, I couldn't convincingly express it. No employer was able to trust me, as I didn't even trust myself very much. When the inevitable question about my salary expectations was asked, I couldn't quote the amount I wanted without hesitating. I often avoided answering this question directly in fear of naming the wrong amount and not getting the job.

I had to take more decisive action. That's when I came across the Baumeister study. After learning about his experiments and reading a series of articles, I was convinced that I needed to practice self-control. The information available to me at the time didn't make it apparent that pornography was harmful and that it was corrupting my behavior and attitude in everyday life, though I suspected that it was to blame. Maybe I didn't want to burden this habit with such blame because I subconsciously didn't want to part ways with it. Nevertheless, after reading Baumeister, I knew I had to give up something powerful, something that I would be sure to miss. I was determined to start controlling myself better. I realized that self-control would define my entire future life.

I decided that I would begin my training by giving up pornography and masturbation completely. As you can imagine, this didn't come easy. Initially, when I knew that I would be in a room alone with a computer, I would mentally prepare myself for avoiding it. Later, however, I forgot about this strategy and quite often returned to my habit. When I came home tired or was hung over, I almost always gave in to the temptation. I remember my frantic thoughts: "I haven't done it in a long time; it won't hurt once in a while," "Everyone does it," and "I have nothing else to do today." This would break my morale and severely distress me. I would even say that I felt depressed after I was done with porn for the evening. Certainly, all of the mechanisms that I described in the previous chapters played a huge part in this. The collapse of my self-confidence also had a profound impact on my mood. I couldn't persevere with my resolution. Fortunately, I didn't give up. As I was constantly struggling to completely stop watching pornography and masturbating, the chemical power of my body was being rebuilt over time, which allowed me to reinforce my willpower. I was slowly beginning to feel that my libido and confidence were returning. Thus, the first positive effects of this decision could be discerned.

After a few relapses on my road to recovery, I found an article about American soldiers in Vietnam who were addicted to heroin en masse.[64] About 40% of the soldiers used heroin, and 20% were addicted to it. These reports shocked the public. Every possible step was taken to heal the war heroes of their addiction, such as opening the Special Action Office of Drug Abuse Prevention. However, to everyone's surprise, when the soldiers returned home, 95% of them quit using heroin, virtually overnight. This information was almost as shocking as the news of their drug abuse. After all, according to statistics, up to 90% of addicts return to their addiction after rehabilitation, whereas the soldiers returning from Vietnam showed that the opposite is true. In Vietnam, they had a number of reasons to turn to hard drugs. The constant risk of battle, the fear of death, the throngs of wounded and dead—all this added up to conditions which were difficult to bear. Life in the barracks forced these men to be surrounded by other heroin

---

[64] Lee N. Robins, Darlene H. Davis, David N. Nurco (1974): *How Permanent Was Vietnam Drug Addiction?*

users and addicts, which is why the addiction spread quickly. Additionally, heroin was cheap and pure in Vietnam, and its ready availability allowed the soldiers to smoke it in joints. Under the conditions of the Vietnam War, soldiers were more vulnerable to the risk of drug addiction. After returning home, their surroundings completely changed. They usually came back to a heroin-free environment, unlike addicts returning from rehab (drug addicts most often return from rehab to the same environment in which they developed the addiction). In the United States, heroin was less available, much more expensive, and of inferior quality, so it had to be injected. Also, there was no war or combat in the new setting, no risk of losing your life, no injured or killed surrounding you. This experience shows that changing one's environment can have a significant impact on heroin use. The number of drug users dropped to a level close to that of the general population. Changing the environment does not guarantee freedom from addiction, but it eliminates the stimuli which push us toward certain behaviors.

Baumeister thinks that it is in fact possible to quit an addiction while one is exposed to the habit-forming stimuli, provided that one's willpower is not burdened with other matters. To quit effectively, you need to concentrate on this goal completely. However, then you would devote all your attention to it and not have the necessary attention for other aspects of life. Therefore, you should instead focus on your circumstances and be especially careful about them. You can arrange your life in such a way so as to avoid opportunities to return to your addiction. You have to do everything in your power to evade the craving and the pressure, because once they appear it will be difficult to stop. We are not strong enough to resist temptation indefinitely. "Your thoughts become words. Your words become actions." If we practice self-control over our thoughts, we can sidestep the need to control our words and deeds.

The story of Vietnam veterans gave me some food for thought. I had to change my surroundings to escape the stimuli that encouraged me to go back to pornography and masturbation, or to even think about them. The first element that I had to completely exclude from my life was sexual stimuli, more specifically, the sight of a female body. Of course, I didn't plan to close my eyes every time I passed a woman on the street or sat in a lecture hall. But I would try not to leer at women in public and not to sexually fantasize about them. I began to steer clear of photos, movies, and any other media that included images of unrealistic women. I stopped watching commercials and admiring the fashion models that I liked so much. All of this had the potential to push me towards pornography and masturbation, and would introduce unnecessary temptation.

The second problem I had to solve definitively was being alone with a computer in a room. First, I moved to another apartment and got rid of my PC, which changed my schedule and habits. I stopped studying at home and went to the library with my textbooks. I did all my research there; I looked for a job and for business ideas there. After class, I didn't go home as usual—I started to alternate between the swimming pool and the gym. I tried to eat out and occasionally cook for myself at home. Soon, however, not having a computer caused problems for me. I had to bring it back. At first, I was able to avoid being alone with it, but evenings and weekends—when the temptation was the largest—still presented a problem.

Then, I came up with a radical idea. I decided to put an extra bed in my room and to offer it to another student. The presence of a roommate kept me away from pornography and masturbation, and saved me some money at the same time. After my ad was published, I quickly found a roommate. I chose someone who seemed intelligent and creative and who I might learn something from. And so, an IT specialist moved in with me and we quickly became friends. Like me, he was looking for business ideas. It proved to be a great decision: we spent a lot of time discussing businesses and looking for new ideas together. He showed me behind the scenes of IT businesses and the world of technology. Those days, start-ups were really booming. The successes of many young inventors fuelled our drive as well. Taking on a roommate turned out to be an excellent decision: it had a positive impact on my development and opened up a new source of knowledge.

The most important thing, though, was that I was able to control my weakness. I didn't waste time and energy on it. When I decided that I was on top of the situation, I began to control other aspects of my life. I decided not to get drunk on the weekends and almost gave up alcohol. I banned snacks from my diet, too, which was also very difficult. I got up and went to bed at the same time every day, allowing myself eight hours of sleep. After a few months, I began to rebuild my natural self-confidence and began to feel that I was the one who in control of my own behavior. My attitude changed. In job interviews, I was much more rational and balanced. Natural self-confidence, newly acquired knowledge, and self-control completely transformed me as a candidate. At that time, I was able to find my dream job in investment banking.

6. FIGHT FOR YOUR RIGHT... OR NEGOTIATE

Let us never negotiate out of fear. But let us never fear to negotiate.

- John F. Kennedy

6.1. THE IMPORTANCE OF ATTITUDE

In the pursuit of a goal, determination is necessary. Assisted by motivation and self-control, it will help us triumph over adversities. We must continue fighting despite failures and setbacks. Sometimes, however, we encounter obstacles on the way to our destination that cannot be overcome. This may present itself as a problem getting our dream job, a distributor's refusal to buy our product, or difficulties in finding an investor for the company, but also as our partner's parents' disapproval of our relationship. We can, however, always continue the conversation and negotiate, which helps to defy the odds, and—sometimes—is the only way out.

Negotiations are an inseparable element of business. It is during negotiations that we most often find out who we are dealing with. That is when one's power of mind and resourcefulness comes to light. Nearly everything is negotiated on a regular basis: from salaries through contracts to payment deadlines—and, in extreme cases, even amounts of tax (or tax relief). This chapter is supposed to be devoted to negotiations. I planned to describe here what negotiations are, what techniques can be used during them, and how to achieve a satisfactory result after them, but there are already many publications about negotiations. On the Internet, you will find practically everything that has ever been said about conducting negotiations. That's why this chapter will deal with something else, namely, the attitude that is necessary for successful negotiations in even the most difficult circumstances. This attitude must be consistently built and maintained, and in order not to lose it we must control ourselves to a high degree and maintain our mental abilities at the highest possible level. A negotiation is one activity which requires exceptional mental fortitude—necessary for quick reactions—as well as unwavering self-confidence.

Erotization, watching pornography, and masturbation, can weaken your negotiating skills. First of all, under the influence of sexual stimuli, the brain is bombarded by large quantities of dopamine, which means that the impact of smaller amounts of dopamine is felt less and less. These small amounts of dopamine are responsible for motivation, which you need also in order to negotiate. Exposure to sexual stimulation before negotiations may result in a lack of drive to negotiate the best result. Put simply: you will not want to negotiate. The same thing can happen when your memory conjures up erotic images or when you are in the company of an attractive woman before or during the negotiations and are aroused sexually. Then, your motivation will focus only on releasing the tension that appears. Therefore, it will be very difficult for you to focus on the subject of the negotiation and on achieving the best possible result.

Another thing is testosterone levels and subjectively perceived testosterone levels. For a man, this hormone is necessary to be able to control himself and to remain self-assured during difficult negotiation talks. Very often, the person with whom we are negotiating tries at all costs to undermine our value and to weaken our position. As a result of excessive masturbation, testosterone levels can drop, which may bring about insecurities and even a feeling of anxiety. Because of this, you will not be able to face the pressure and you will adopt a defensive posture and mindset; thus, it will be much more difficult for you to reach a satisfactory agreement. During negotiations, we will often attempt to strengthen our negotiating position—whether through a suitable technique, or even through a bluff—to achieve a better result. At the same time, we need to control our posture and body language so as not to reveal our true emotions. It is thanks to a high testosterone level and our self-control skills that we will be able to stick to our bottom line until the end by keeping a poker face.

Sexual stimuli can cause our general motivation to decrease significantly. Ambitious goals will seem unfeasible. In addition, these stimuli can make us much more likely to make concessions. Businessmen around the world know that one negotiating session can often affect the entire business, and that's why they pay so much attention to negotiating skills. It's not unheard-of for a few hours of negotiations to involve more intellectual effort than some other activity over years of work. Interestingly, the nature of the entire relationship with a potential contractor is usually established during the negotiations, so one's negotiating position must be permanently maintained. When negotiating, we usually encounter an intellect as powerful as ours or even more so, which is also trying to get the best deal. If our goal is to succeed in business, we must take extra care of our mind in order to achieve this. How effectively we control ourselves and how confidently we feel will translate into how successful we are in negotiations, in business, and in life as a whole.

You won't acquire negotiating skills by reading brief guides and "useful tips." You need to gain experience by negotiating a lot and for increasingly higher stakes. Yet, you can considerably speed up your learning process by being aware of key aspects during your first major negotiations. Negotiations strongly affect the shape of our lives. We can negotiate for employment, a better salary, and a lower cost of living. Unfortunately, people often do not pay much attention to negotiations and allow themselves to suffer losses. In addition, they consider negotiations to be exhausting and irrelevant. They think, "Why burden our heads and argue with someone for god knows how long when we can agree to their terms right away and relax instead?" Others don't wish to be a source of disappointment for other people. If the other party doesn't get a good deal, they will be sad or even upset. This may cause some discomfort in people who are not trained in negotiating techniques. This approach is disastrous and characteristic of impatient people. Still others avoid negotiating because of a lack of motivation, which was lost for various reasons: when the reward system is abused, for example.

I'm not saying that you have to negotiate everywhere you go. Negotiating in everyday situations, such as with your barber or at a restaurant, can be seen as bad manners. On the other hand, in some cultures, mainly Arabic ones, you almost always have to negotiate—and to do it hard enough not to get cheated. You need to know how important the subject of the transaction is and how harmful it would be for you not to negotiate. Often, by negotiating for only a few dollars we only waste our precious time. We certainly negotiate when seeking employment in a new place, in business, when we buy a car or house, or when we rent an apartment. In my opinion, it is also worth negotiating smaller purchases, such as electronics or furniture, or when renting a vacation home.

In many situations, the justification for negotiations is age. It is assumed that young people have little or no income at all. You should use this privilege, if only for the sake of practice. It is also worth paying attention to whether the other party is versed in negotiating techniques. If they are, it will certainly not be a problem for them to start negotiations. Unfortunately, if we don't practice negotiating, then—when we are forced to do so—it is very likely that we won't manage as well as we'd like to. Negotiations consist of many elements, such as emotions, tricks, and persuasiveness, and only by practicing will we be able to deal with them.

6.2. SELF-CONTROL IN NEGOTIATIONS

When I was in college, I sometimes went shopping in a grocery store near the apartment where I was living. The owner set the prices high, so I only made my purchases there in exceptional situations. In fact, it's tough to say what prices he charged because each time I was there, they were different. The more I rushed through my shopping, the higher the prices he quoted. He would even charge several times more for the same goods than the store nearby. In the end, I started to treat my trips to his store like training in negotiating. When I was looking for business ideas, I had a good idea of the wholesale prices of various products and I was able to estimate how much the shopkeeper marked up various goods. It made me feel more confident. One time, he demanded $9 for a can of cola, a bag of rice, and a few tomatoes. Imagine how surprised he was when I told him, "Four dollars or I'm going somewhere else." He didn't budge; he only shook his head. I turned towards the exit and as I crossed the threshold, he called out, "Six dollars!" I didn't concede, of course, but walked the few hundred yards to the next store. From that point on, he quoted me more reasonable prices, and even seemed to have gained some respect for me.

Negotiations like this can be a sort of training lesson, but due to my strong negotiating position, they hardly required any effort. In this situation, I wasn't forced to take his offer because I could always walk a bit further to another store or even if I paid those few dollars more, it wouldn't have been a problem. My negotiating position, therefore, was very good; the shopkeeper's was slightly weaker, considering that he was running a corner grocery store on a street with little foot traffic and probably had to support his whole family.

The negotiating skills that I want to talk about are applicable to situations in which our negotiating position is significantly worse than the other party's position. For example: we are interviewing for our dream job. We don't have much experience in that profession, 10 candidates are competing for a single vacancy, and we still want to negotiate a suitable salary. There is no doubt that in this case a weak negotiating position will lead to an unsatisfactory result and may even prevent us from taking part in any negotiations. Most people in the job market have found themselves in a similar situation at least once in their lives. So, how do you convince a recruiter that you are the right candidate and how do you land that job with a good salary? Of course, you can—and even have to—show your best side, in other words, respond well to their questions, display your intelligence and eagerness to work, and hide that fact that if you get a better offer elsewhere, you won't hesitate to take it. However, if 10 candidates are vying for the position, it's very likely that the majority of them will also demonstrate similar characteristics. So how do you get an edge and gain the trust of a recruiter?

Although negotiating employment and future compensation is usually a small part of the interview, we must treat the whole meeting as the underpinning of these negotiations. This applies not only to interviews, but to all other negotiations, and even situations in which we must present our credentials. The attitude we choose during these conversations is the key factor. Note that we always prefer the people who seem confident, have self-esteem, and look as if they are following a plan. Most often, we can tell that they are determined to achieve their goal and that they know how to do it, while for us such a goal remains unattainable. Such people easily win others over. They are also sought after for the highest-paid positions, for example, those which require contact with major clients of the company or involve the acquisition of significant contracts. This will become our attitude if we set ourselves ambitious long-term goals and meet them.

It is also important to be trustworthy and—under the most difficult conditions and in unfavorable circumstances—to keep your cool and do what is best at the moment. Such people are distinguished by their even-tempered emotionality: they react equally to both good and bad messages, are assertive and resistant to self-suggestion, and deal with information flowing from the environment selectively. This behavior also requires a lot of self-control. You may think it is a well-known truth that self-confident people do better in their lives. The key is to take care of the body's natural strength, which will make you feel confident. Men definitely find it easier to maintain such an attitude with a high, uninterrupted level of testosterone. Thanks to testosterone, they can also control themselves well and they remain calm in difficult circumstances.

What should we do when our hormone economy is rebuilt, we have set long-term goals, and our attitude is greatly improved? It should also be mentioned that having the knowledge necessary to hold a given job or the market knowledge necessary for negotiation will boost our confidence. What's more, if the subject of negotiation is employment, we can find out beforehand what the average salary for a similar position is, what returns the employer gets from the work of such an employee, and what the margin of profitability of such a job may be. If these are business negotiations, we can additionally do research on the other party, for example, find out what stage of business they are at, what prices they previously bought or sold similar goods or services, or what financial means are available to them.

Most importantly, however, there are ways to effectively elevate our negotiating position with self-control. One of them is to set ourselves a current goal higher than necessary. For example, if we want to work in Company X for $60,000 a year and this is achievable, but at the same time we expect an offer of $50,000 dollars, then we must behave as if we were shooting for $70,000 a year. Why would this attitude change anything? When the target is set higher than expected, the attitude changes automatically and we are more likely to be more ambitious. The reward system stimulates us with a higher dose of dopamine. It improves our cognitive abilities, sharpens our mind, and generally brings out our strengths, which manifest in the face of difficult challenges and validate us as a solid candidate for the job, as well as garnering more respect from people. The crucial aspect of this method is the fact that when we later come down from our target figure closer to the expected offer—either during the negotiations or in the game going on in our mind—our attitude will be a clear indication to the other party that we are making a big concession. This behavior will suggest that we are committed to mutual success, which may encourage the other side to compromise.

According to a meta-analysis of 22 studies conducted by

Zetik and Suthlmacher,[65] setting yourself high objectives or challenges during negotiations translates into higher profits than objectives which are too low or missing. The size of the challenge has a significant impact on the outcome of the negotiations. Higher goals lead to better results. The researchers mention four cases in which setting a goal has an even stronger effect:
- when the other party hasn't set a challenging goal,
- when there is a fixed reward for the result of negotiations,
- when the negotiations do not take place face to face, and
- when the negotiator is experienced.

It isn't important who sets the goal for the negotiation. This means that setting your own goal is not fundamentally different from situations where the goal is set by your superior, for example, and it has the same impact on reaching the goal. As I mentioned, sexual stimuli may lower your expectations of the negotiation, which will translate into a much weaker negotiating stance and a poorer outcome. Also, too much exposure to sexual stimuli that are not real male–female relationships can sink your self-esteem.

According to another method of strengthening your negotiating position, one should think of a good or better alternative. For example, if we are fighting for the job in Company X for $60,000 a year, and we expect an offer of $50,000, we must remember that Company Y also has a job for $50,000 a year. If there is no real alternative on offer, then we should take into account the entire job market, where we can earn $50,000 in any job, assuming that this figure is close to the market average and there is no pressure to sign a contract at any cost. With such a conviction, we will additionally know our own value, and

---

[65] Deborah C. Zetik, Alice F. Stuhlmacher (2002): *Goal Setting and Negotiation Performance: A Meta-Analysis*.

so the recruiter will value us higher as well. Having a real alternative during negotiations realistically improves our negotiating stance.

A very good way of preparing for negotiations is considering different scenarios and planning possible reactions to them. It is always advisable to prepare a contingency plan in case the talks don't go our way. When we get confused and lose confidence, it will be difficult for us to come up with a strategy to rebuild our position. This will be much easier if we prepare a plan of action in advance for such circumstances.

Another method that will help bolster our negotiating position is mental contrasting, or positive thinking about the future. Although it is not a negotiation strategy, it is a more manipulative approach that requires a great deal of self-control. Specifically, our attitude will dramatically improve if we are convinced that we can ensure a satisfying future and a happy life for ourselves. Thanks to such an optimistic attitude, we will feel more self-confident and we will be perceived as such by the other party. A healthy dose of optimism is recommended not only during negotiations. Unfortunately, a mind which is often exposed to intense sexual stimuli tends to suggest to us that any risk or minor failure in life will bring on a huge catastrophe, which is usually not true.

There are plenty of negotiating techniques requiring increased self-control and I encourage you to explore them. Keep in mind, however, that their effectiveness is directly proportional to one's skills of self-control, level of self-confidence, and overall condition of body and mind. The main methods which allow for a better negotiating position seem banal, but—believe me—in a stressful situation it is easy to forget about them and to return to the belief that our negotiating position is weak and that the only thing we should present to the other party is humility. That's why self-control and naturally built self-confidence are so essential during negotiations. Unfortunately, for someone who is not very well-controlled, who suffers from reduced testosterone levels, or is troubled by any other uncertainties, this attitude will be much harder to maintain. We must remember that the negotiation process often stretches beyond one meeting, so there may be many opportunities for you to give in. Admittedly, during negotiations in exceptional situations, it is possible to change your negotiation strategy, but a sudden abandonment of your original assumptions will usually spoil your image and end in failure.

You may doubt the effectiveness of these methods or wonder whether it's possible to improve your negotiating position with self-control. The researchers Jager, Loschelder, and Friese explored the possibility of overcoming a weak negotiating stance by means of self-control.[66] They performed tests using simulated negotiations, in which a total of 861 respondents took part. The tests were carried out face-to-face and via computer. The participants were assigned one of four different negotiating positions: a good negotiating position, a weak negotiating position, a weak negotiating position supported by a set goal,[67] and a weak position supported by a contingency plan.[68] Both methods of supporting a weak negotiating position required the participants to display

---

[66] Andreas Jäger, David D. Loschelder, Malte Friese (2017): *Using Self-regulation to Successfully Overcome the Negotiation Disadvantage of Low Power.*

[67] The studied subject was given a goal, for example, "Be persistent and achieve the highest score possible."

[68] What I have in mind is the if-then method, i.e., when suitable circumstances emerge, we act according to the appropriate plan. For example, "If I receive a low offer, I will reject it and counter-offer with a compromise" or "If my opponent puts pressure on me, I will not lose my cool but will present my offer in small steps."

self-control and to follow the instructions they were given. The face-to-face negotiations were connected with a contract for the purchase and sale of equipment, and the negotiations via computer were about a job. As expected, in both cases the good negotiating position brought much better results than the weak negotiating position.[69] On the other hand, to the astonishment of the researchers, in both the case of face-to-face negotiations and negotiations over the computer, the weak negotiating positions supported by a goal or a contingency plan yielded results that were close to those from the good negotiating position—or even better. The participants with a weak negotiating position usually made many more conciliatory offers than those with a strong position. The participants with a weak position supported by self-control methods submitted more ambitious offers. Analysis of this study showed that self-control increased the respondents' resistance from the very beginning of the negotiations. There is no doubt that the use of self-control methods helped the participants to overcome the weakness associated with a low negotiating position. Thanks to the self-control tools used in the experiment, the participants with little negotiating power:

- made offers which were more focused on their own benefits,
- paid less attention to the needs of the other party,
- rejected the weak offers of the opponents more easily, and
- resisted the temptation to make large and premature concessions.

Research shows that despite the obvious benefits of using this type of support, people lacking in strength have difficulty implementing even simple goal-oriented activities. When approaching negotiations, we often even subconsciously underestimate our own negotiating position,

---

[69] In each case, the mean score of the results was reported.

which generates poorer results. It should be remembered that the participants weren't subject to any risk from taking part in the research. Admittedly, an appropriate reward was set to motivate them, but the responsibility they assumed was in no way equivalent to the responsibility borne in real negotiations. Therefore, note that with the growth of responsibility and higher stakes, self-control and self-confidence skills must be correspondingly greater. Often, an opponent for whom the stakes are relatively low will find it much easier to gain an advantage over someone for whom the stakes are relatively high, although this may seem counter-intuitive. If we care about something, we can be much more susceptible to the stress surrounding the negotiations and may lose control. The opponent's freedom to act will help them maintain their confidence, which can knock us off track if we don't have enough confidence. In addition, those who negotiate regularly feel much more self-assured at the negotiating table. Their experience allows them to predict their opponent's moves. They are taught which reactions to expect from different techniques and it is difficult to surprise them. Most often, opponents with little experience are easy prey for such negotiators.

    A lack of experience in negotiations doesn't play such a large role during a job interview, as recruiters see the course of negotiations in two ways. On the one hand, they are negotiating for the most effective contract for the employer, while on the other hand they are closely observing the candidate's behavior during the negotiations. They assess his or her reliability, so the candidate's firm stance often works favorably. However, in the case of business negotiations, the most common goal is to make the most profit, so by negotiating without experience, self-control, and patience, we risk losing a lot. A good example of this is young service providers with little experience who have to fight for every commission. They are often employed by large clients. Big players know very well that companies which have been on the market longer value their services higher, although their performance is rarely different. Understanding the situation of these smaller companies, they will place much lower offers. The young companies will often accept the job, which may barely cover their own costs. It will take a long time before they become practiced in negotiating contracts. For a young company, each new contract is a big deal, while the client usually doesn't care too much about who provides the service. It has to be the right quality and—if possible—cheap, so they feel free to bring the price down to a minimum. Negotiations will take place in the life of all entrepreneurs in the end, especially in the services sector, which is why the ability to negotiate and rehearsing your attitude at the negotiating table is so important.

6.3. THE FUTURE IS NEGOTIABLE

In my career, I learned the hard way about the importance of negotiations. Unfortunately, I paid for my ignorance out of my own pocket. During my first job interview in auditing, I was paralyzed when asked about my income expectations. At that time, I knew nothing about building a negotiating attitude, and to make matters worse, I continued to regularly watch porn and masturbate. My testosterone level was barely perceptible, and the same was true for my motivation, but the fear of rejection was the hardest to overcome. Luckily for me, large consulting companies usually have an established structure of earnings for low-level employees and these earnings are often well-known in the academic community. I hesitantly told the recruiter the expected rate, which I had heard from my friends, and, dejected, I awaited the impending doom. All that time, I was convinced that I didn't deserve such money, especially because I did poorly in the interview. What's more, the salary for a junior assistant in auditing were close to the national average, which was almost unattainable in the county I come from.

When I was offered the job and the contract included the amount I had quoted, it seemed to me that I was born under a lucky star. Nothing could wipe the joy and excitement off of my face. This was another critical symptom of the hopeless attitude that I had adopted. A symptom of zero self-control and showing your hand to your opponent. I submitted to such extreme emotions that if the recruiter had changed her mind, I would most likely have burst into tears.

It's necessary to control ourselves when we are in a bad position, but it is even more important to control ourselves when our position is good. It is true that after I signed the contract there was nothing more to do, but in negotiations you must never reveal your bottom line. After all, if I were to extend my contract with this employer, she might remember that I was delighted by merely signing a contract, and the next time might offer me worse terms than my colleagues in similar positions. My ignorance may have also made me care so much about getting that job. When I learned about the duties of an assistant auditor, the joy of signing the contract quickly evaporated. Most senior assistants and seniors employees were not exactly burning with passion, either, which discouraged me even more. So it wasn't only that my attitude was bad, but that I hadn't prepared myself for the job interview at all. I hadn't checked whether this kind of work would suit me or what sacrifices I would be making. It was good for me to gain a lot of experience there, but, unfortunately, I hadn't drawn any conclusions from those interviews and negotiations yet.

In my first business steps, there was also little room for negotiations. As far as the crepe cart and the distribution of T-shirts went, I dictated the terms, which I mainly came up with out of nowhere. When I was running an online business, I negotiated more often, but these were negotiations via email correspondence and most often concerned granting small discounts on the posted items.

I only got a real lesson in negotiating when I was

employed in investment banking. As I mentioned, it took me a long time to find my dream job. Until then, I went to very many job interviews; while my sense of self-worth continued to plummet, I nonetheless felt like nothing could crush my spirits even more. It is worth mentioning that I had already quit pornography, so my attitude had improved considerably. The bank I applied to as a financial analyst was one of many smaller banks on the market. It handled small and medium-sized transactions, but its previous business had allowed it to consolidate its position. Before the interview, I did my homework and learned about the bank's greatest accomplishments and about its clients. I made sure not to show that I was stressed but to behave casually. I was being interviewed by one of the senior managers, Jack, whose team I was to join in the end. He greeted me amicably, and most of the conversation was conducted this way. I answered the questions correctly and fairly. I made a good impression during the part about the company's prior achievements, as I demonstrated my expertise and conveyed my knowledge of the market. Although I had a hunch that we were getting along fairly well, my limited experience in the industry still kept me from feeling too confident. In addition, I had seen the other candidates in the hallway.

When the subject of salary came up in the conversation, the friendly atmosphere suddenly vanished. The manager was stony-faced and from then on, scrutinized me closely, without so much as blinking. At that moment, for the first time, I had the opportunity to witness what a good negotiating stance looks like. It was the first time I had seen a professional at work. At first I felt confused; after all, we had just been chatting so warmly. In time, I remembered that it would depend on my attitude whether I seemed suitable for the job. Following Jack's lead, I also became serious and I presented the matter like this: "I want to work in investment banking but I have no experience, which is why I will make a concession in the form of lower salary during the 3-month probationary period. But if I prove myself, then I will expect to earn a normal salary after this period." It seemed to me that these words were the most appropriate at the moment. On the one hand, I sounded confident, and on the other hand I made a significant concession. After such a response, I expected to see approval in the facial expression of my recruiter. Nothing could be further from the truth. Jack noted down the figure I quoted, thanked me for my time, and said goodbye. It took a lot of effort for me to maintain my professionalism and to say goodbye without stammering. As I was leaving, I saw the next candidate waiting for his turn. The interview had exhausted me mentally, and this was just the beginning. In hindsight, I can say that I simply chickened out and valued myself too little, but considering how much I cared about that job then, I had behaved correctly. Although I had left myself an open door to renegotiate the contract in three months' time, it wasn't certain whether the next negotiation would go my way.

    The next day I received a phone call saying that I had made a good impression at the interview and that I was invited to meet with the director. Exultant, I went to the second interview, thinking that it would be only a formality. In the director's office, however, I wasn't warmly greeted by a gray-haired man welcoming me to the company. The director of the bank was Frank—a big, fat, bald man about fifty years old, with Italian roots. When I walked into his office, he was talking on the phone and pretended not to see me. He didn't reply to my "good morning," either. This immediately killed my enthusiasm. After a long while, Frank put down the phone and began boring into me with his squinting eyes, waiting for me to lose the rest of my self-confidence. He was just like a policeman interrogating a suspect. It was only after a long time that he told me to introduce myself and say something about myself. When I was going over my résumé point by point, he asked me about my academic knowledge. He questioned each of my answers, regardless of how confident of them I was. The shakier my voice got, the more satisfaction I saw on his face. About halfway through this strange conversation, I realized that I was being tested. Only then did I begin to defend my opinions, although it didn't matter anymore. Frank said he wasn't convinced, but since Jack thought I was a good fit he would let me prove myself during the trial period. It's a start, I thought. I was still warned that I would be monitored and that I should be prepared for another interview in three months' time. I left satisfied. In the end, I was offered the position of a financial analyst and I had gotten a foot in the door of investment banking. I didn't know, however, that Frank was playing a negotiating game with me.

During the probationary period, I gave it everything I had. I worked a lot of overtime in the office, and I even managed to pull all-nighters: that's the beauty of this industry. Jack was pleased with my work, and my financial models and presentations made it through to meetings with investors without major amendments. Two weeks before the end of my trial period, Frank called me into his office. I read dissatisfaction on his face. He looked at me for a moment and growled, "For now we are content with your work, but it could be better. We'll extend your contract and give you a 15% pay raise." This was the so-called low-ball offer. When I heard that I would only get a 15% raise, it completely threw me off. I knew that the market average was twice my current pay. I was stumped and I had no idea how to respond. Frank was still looking at me, disappointed, enjoying the thought that I was squirming with rage. I only said that it wasn't enough; that was all the courage I could muster. I still lacked the strength to steadfastly refuse this offer, even though I had much more experience by then. Frank casually asked me how much I wanted, to which I timidly replied 50% more. He winced even more and said, "You have two weeks left until the end of your contract, so I have some time to think about it." I left the office angry and confused. I still wasn't very self-controlled. My mind was so racked by emotions that my head ached.

I decided that I couldn't wait for Frank's response and that I had to start looking for another job. While browsing the ads, I noticed one for my position, published a few hours after my interview with Frank. I was devastated. It was understandable that Frank wanted a back-up plan in case we couldn't agree, just like I wanted to send some résumés. However, I couldn't control myself and lapsed into paranoia. I kept telling myself that I couldn't lose this job, which was very stupid of me. Every night without an answer was another sleepless night. Then I did the worst thing possible: I couldn't stand it any longer, so after a week I told Frank that I accepted his low-ball offer. The boss naturally took advantage of the fact that I had given in, and proposed one more probationary period under the current conditions, judging my attitude to be incomprehensible. I accepted his offer in a frenzy. This has proven to be the biggest negotiation lesson in my life.

Looking back at this now, I would not have renewed the contract with myself if I had been in Frank's shoes. It was only after that conversation that I understood the importance of negotiating skills—after showing a complete lack of them. Although my hormonal economy was recovering, I still had no experience of how to behave in stressful situations. My first important negotiation took place at a time when I should have already been well-prepared for it. Unfortunately, the time that I could have devoted to overcoming character-building difficulties was wasted watching people copulating. I couldn't stand a conversation going on in a vacuum because that vacuum overwhelmed me too quickly. I was able to fashion the appearance of a poised man, but it still wasn't enough, if only because Frank had me in the palm of his hand, and I couldn't keep my emotions in check. I hadn't forgotten that I started working in investment banking in order to gain business experience, and—as you may have noticed—from Jack, Frank, and the entire team from the office, I really had a lot to learn, starting with the art of negotation.

I went through the next probationary period the same way as the first one, except that I was already working on many projects and had a lot of responsibility. This time I did research on negotiating techniques, including those which I described at the beginning of the chapter. In addition, I re-enrolled in the university bridge club. Bridge was played there only officially—in fact, poker ruled there. When I first started college, I visited the club in search of additional excitement when pornography and masturbation bored me. It usually took a lot of nerve and money, so I soon parted ways with that group. I knew the rules of the game very well, but I wasn't able to control myself enough to outsmart other players. Every bluff or large bet I went to make paralyzed and automatically compromised me. I couldn't wait patiently and made rash decisions instead. Playing poker is excellent training in negotiation skills: it practices, among other things, self-confidence, patience, putting yourself at risk, pretending not to take any risk—bluffing—and keeping a poker face. The student organization was not about gambling or putting on a high-stakes game, but it was aimed at training ourselves at this respectable game. There was never more than a few dozen dollars on the table because our college student budgets didn't allow for it. On the other hand, playing poker without money is pointless. The greatest joy for me was the battle of minds and rankings, and the game itself became iconic once several graduates became professional players.

When I first returned to the club, the game still caused me great discomfort. It was hard for me to get used my stack of my chips growing and then suddenly melting away to almost nothing. In the beginning, I lost tens of dollars, but after several poker sessions I was able to finish with some earnings. It was much easier for me to control myself when I didn't watch porn or masturbate. The fear that had once accompanied me while betting had now disappeared. When playing poker, you can avoid risk and not lose, but it's hard to win anything this way. The big lesson I learned from poker was to assess and take moderate risks, but most importantly, I finally started to feel comfortable doing so.

Before my next talk with my boss, I felt different. I was prepared. My stress level was much lower and my expectations were higher. I prepared a number of arguments and strategies for dealing with Frank's various moves. I assumed that I wanted to earn 100% more than before, but following the method of the highest goal, I decided to fight for 140%. Considering that I had spent half a year working for peanuts, my expectations were not too high: this salary didn't differ from the salaries of analysts with one year of experience.

To my surprise, Frank took a different approach this time. Now he approached me as a colleague, pleased by my presence. He said that my attitude had changed for the better and that he wanted to keep me on for longer. He offered me an open-ended contract and a 50% raise. He was sure that I would be excited about his offer like each previous time. I had prepared myself for such a move—I had a plan of action. I withheld my answer for a long time and watched Frank with a straight face. When I noticed the confusion on his face, I presented a series of arguments. I brought up my commitment in the office and the fact that Jack was happy with my work. I also added that in the meantime I had done some research on typical salaries. I said that I felt offended that I had worked so long for such a low salary, even though my work was flawless and had translated into a number of profitable transactions for the bank. I told Frank that if he wanted me to stay with them, I would require compensation: I would normally demand a 100% increase, but in this situation I expected 140%.

Frank was quite dismayed to hear these words. He knew now that he was on the back foot. A few key transactions depended heavily on me, and—apart from Jack—only I was able to take care of them. Training another analyst would cause a huge delay and risk torpedoing the whole project, and hiring an experienced analyst who could instantly take over my projects would involve even greater costs. It was two weeks till the end of my contract, and Frank again asked for time to think about it. I refused. I boldly stated that I would wait no more than 24 hours for an answer and that if they didn't make me a suitable offer, I would use my vacation days to finish out the current contract. I felt afraid; I knew that I was exaggerating and that my expectations were too high, and that my behavior was almost indecent, but I didn't show it. Frank only saw that I was incensed by his attitude. When I left his office, Jack was immediately called for a meeting. I couldn't wait around for the result of the conversation because my work day was over. My head was very muddled, but I did everything not to think about work. I went straight from the office to the bridge club and I forgot about the conversation for the whole evening.

The following day, an open-ended employment contract was lying on my desk granting me a 120% pay raise. Jack only said that it was all they could offer right now. I agreed. I didn't have another conversation with Frank, but when he walked through the office, I could see a grimace on his face. I felt guilty all the time. My demands were unethical at a time when Frank and Jack were cornered. Then I remembered that they didn't hesitate to take advantage of my weakness. These negotiations did not affect my relationship with Jack, while Frank began to treat me with more respect. Only then did I feel like a full member of the staff and I was able to do my job without my insecurities.

In investment banking, you gain experience very quickly because there is a lot of work to be done. After a few months, I started to participate in meetings with investors. It was only then that I saw negotiations at the highest level, with tens of millions of dollars hanging on the attitude of the investors. The investment bank in which I worked was famous on the market for leading uncompromising negotiations. Jack and Frank could sell very expensive companies with dubious futures, while paying very little for companies with solid fundamentals. They were adventurous and they often ostentatiously broke off negotiations in order to seal the deal after a few months on their own terms. They used time masterfully. They knew when to play for time, and when there was no time to waste. At any given moment, they had a series of indisputable arguments that emphasized their claims. They conquered customers' trust very easily. They held a vast store of experience that they were happy to share at any opportunity. Their attitude was most often impeccable. They controlled themselves and never gave in to their emotions. Usually, they set the negotiating goal very high and sought to achieve it without any qualms. After such an experience, I had no doubt that in order to maintain such an intellectual condition and such negotiating skills, I couldn't under any circumstances expose myself to stimuli that would rob me of my attention and cause me to hesitate.

My job at the investment bank was very educational. Whereas working in auditing focused on clients' books, the bank had much more insight into the companies they did transactions with. This work required not only a thorough, discerning look at the finances and operations of the companies, but it was also important to have the ability to make real financial planning based on predictions. You might think what I'm saying is odd, but I have found that people who are good at forecasting the future perform the best on the investment market. The best investors in the world are those who freely move around in a future timeframe and even dedicate most of their attention to the future. Initially, this is associated with exceptional discomfort. Someone who enters the world of serious investments for the first time may think that he or she is in the company of lunatics, and instinctively want to return to normalcy. How can anyone who bets unimaginably large assets on dubious analyses and projections be normal? It's difficult to take seriously long-term economic projections and prognoses of the behavior of companies, especially since these are based on questionable analyses, dependent on the assumptions of fallible people. Nevertheless, the truth is that unless our mind learns to operate freely in the future, we will not have any chance of success in investing.

This type of prognostication of the future which I'm talking about has nothing to do with divination by tea leaves, fortune tellers, or tarot cards. Basically, success in predicting the future—that is, the aforementioned analyzes and forecasts—depends on one's breadth of knowledge and experience, just as creativity consists of a synthesis of existing information. In other words, the more knowledge and experience we acquire, the more accurate our predictions will be and the more we will be able to rely on them. An excellent way to practice predicting the future is to play chess, which is largely based on anticipating several moves in advance. However, looking forward is not everything. It's also about monetizing your forecasts, or in other words, betting on future scenarios. This is the most difficult element of stepping into the future. In order to be able to do it, we need courage, self-confidence, self-control, the ability to deal with risk, and acceptance of the possibility of failure. To maintain such an attitude, which is desirable when investing, it's necessary to retain a steady hormone economy and a naturally functioning reward system. It is thanks to this that we will not be afraid to take a step into the unknown. On the other hand, exposure to supernormal stimuli will undermine our natural predispositions and weaken many necessary bodily functions, which will not allow for effective investing.

7. GETTING ACCUSTOMED TO RISK

Fortune favors the brave.

— *Virgil*

7.1. THE BRIGHT SIDE OF UNCERTAINTY

Experienced investors know that risk is an inherent element of every investment. Most of them can assess the risk and the likelihood of implementing the planned project. There are even whole branches of science devoted to managing and controlling risk. Each major bank has a department dedicated to assessing the risk of all the assets in their portfolio. Most market participants also use ratings set by specialized agencies, which provide indicators of risk for various entities and financial instruments. The issue of risk is closely connected with the statistics and with probability theory and is ubiquitous in broadly understood business. One of the areas related to investing which is directly linked to statistics, probability and risk, is financial engineering. Used to build various econometric/financial models that aid in effective investing, it accurately crunches the future into numbers. I encourage you to look into this valuable and very comprehensive field, which has already been studied by many researchers. I, in turn, will focus again on the attitude that is necessary to take risk. What I want to mention here is most often addressed in books on investment psychology. It is a state of mind, an emotional balance that cannot be disturbed when making difficult decisions. This issue is well-known among traders: how well they control their emotions is usually reflected in their success in trading.

Although the topic is most often explored by investors and speculators, it is of great importance throughout our lives. Risk accompanies us not only in investing and in business, but also in tough, crucial life choices. Contrary to what one might think, most professional investors are not trained in risk assessment and in probability theory. As one gains more and more experience, risk assessment and probability estimation become instinctive and easily grasped. Also, in the course of the development of the human brain, this ability is unconsciously exercised when we are exposed to risk at an early age. It is when we encounter our first difficulties in life and try to overcome them on our own that we develop the ability to deal with risk. We practiced it, for example, by conquering the fear of public appearances at school, when someone bullied us and we found the courage to stand up to them, and when we received a bad grade at school and admitted it to our parents. Unfortunately, the fewer difficult situations we face in life, the less experience we have in controlling ourselves. What's worse, the more pleasure we provide for ourselves, the worse our body will react to any unpleasantness. The same applies to watching pornography and masturbation and the artificial, intense pleasure that they produce. By overindulging in easy and quick pleasures, we don't give ourselves the chance to experience situations that expose us to risk and to the stress that comes with it, or we even deliberately avoid such situations. Unfortunately, if we haven't experienced much risk, it will be difficult to bear in the future. What's more, systematic pornography use and masturbation are highly likely to disrupt the hormonal balance and the production of testosterone—the hormone which helps men to maintain control over themselves and their actions, in difficult situations. Therefore, when our hormonal economy is out of whack, every exposure to risk can be accompanied by panic and fear, which are not conducive to making good decisions, especially when each failure brings on intense depressive symptoms. Avoiding risky situations that cause discomfort deprives us of the possibility to gather experience related to risk. This, in turn, means that we won't feel confident in many areas of life and we will consciously avoid making responsible decisions, such as changing a job, buying a house, or starting a family. Perhaps we subconsciously want fulfillment in life, but our body keeps us in a safe area, commonly referred to as one's comfort zone. Unfortunately, resorting to easy and simple pleasures may rob us of the chance to experience truly beautiful moments.

    The key is to understand the risk involved, to accept it, and to be able to sacrifice what we now have—something that is certain and available—in the name of a much greater but uncertain benefit. What comes into play here is motivation and prioritization, which were described in the previous chapters, along with the fact that a body submitted to frequent eroticization, pornography, and masturbation may fear any unpredictability. A healthy body and a healthy hormonal balance help you to overcome fear and to pursue your dreams. Most often, the first, most important step towards happiness requires the greatest courage and risk. Don't get me wrong—taking risks doesn't mean gambling in a casino. You probably recognize that even spending one's time and youth studying for classes is a risk, because in the future we may not gain the earnings and satisfaction we expected, despite our education. In the same way, by trusting another person and investing our feelings in him or her toward build a happy relationship, we risk desolation and a broken heart. If we decide to sacrifice our lives and go on a mission in developing countries to help disadvantaged people, we risk our health, for example. Everything that can bring happiness and fulfillment in life is associated with a certain risk.

Investments and the road to material wealth is fraught with the most palpable risk. Every experienced businessman knows that success is almost always associated with risking one's resources and time. Regardless of the industry, this rule always applies. Whether it is on capital markets, or in traditional commodity trading, or in the provision of services, in order to achieve success, you must take risk (of course, according to your knowledge of a given market), but also try to minimize it as much as possible. You can't succeed in business without taking the first step, and that requires courage. Even then, a stable hormone balance which warrants the right attitude and determination is requisite. Having a body in good condition will help you feel more confident and more comfortable when you need to take risks, and will also help you come to terms with a possible loss.

7.2. RESEARCH ON RISK-TAKING

The first large study on more than 2,000 pornography viewers showed a close relationship between the use of pornography and aversion to risk.[70] A longer period of abstinence was associated with a greater appetite for risk. One of the reasons for this correlation is that pornography leads to physical changes in the brain. Research has shown that frequent pornography viewing negatively affects the amount of gray matter and the activity of selected brain areas, as well as weakening some functional connections in the brain.[71] As it turns out,[72] the same areas of the human brain are largely responsible for risk propensity.

Another reason is the negative impact of pornography on testosterone levels in men, which is closely correlated with a disposition toward risk. Research on the influence of hormones on investment behavior have been generating a lot of attention for a long time. It was soon observed that testosterone doesn't only affect a man's reproductive functions and the search for a partner. In 2007, researchers affiliated with Harvard University examined the effect of testosterone levels on one's willingness to take risks.[73] The study included 98 men who were tested for testosterone levels. The subjects were then examined for risk

---

[70] The study was conducted as a survey among users of the website nofap.com, a community focused on helping to fight addiction to pornography.
http://www.alec-sproten.eu/language/en/2016/01/18/how-abstinence-affects-preferences/

[71] Simone Kühn, PhD; Jürgen Gallinat, PhD (2014): *Brain Structure and Functional Connectivity Associated With Pornography Consumption: The Brain on Porn.*

[72] Hengyi Rao, Marc Korczykowski, John Pluta, Angela Hoang, John A. Detre (2008): *Neural correlates of voluntary and involuntary risk taking in the human brain: An fMRI Study of the Balloon Analog Risk Task (BART).*

[73] Coren L. Apicella, Anna Dreber, Benjamin Campbell, Peter B. Gray, Moshe Hoffman, Anthony C. Little (2008): *Testosterone and financial risk preferences.*

propensity. Everyone received $250 and was asked to decide how much of this amount they would allocate for a risky investment. The participant was allowed to keep the rest of the money. This risky investment was a coin toss. In the event of a win, the return was two and a half times the amount wagered; in the event of a loss, the participant would lose all the money he had wagered. If the subject decided to keep the full $250, he was assigned the lowest possible risk-taking classification, and if he decided to bet everything, he was classified among the highest possible risk-taking group. The results of the study clearly showed that risk seeking correlates with the level of testosterone. The higher the testosterone level in the subject, the greater the amount he risked. The results of the study also indicate the economic significance of the influence of testosterone on risk seeking. According to the researchers, one standard deviation of testosterone level produced an investment $17 higher than the average.

Perhaps, as the authors of the study claim, men evolved to engage in riskier activities. Natural predispositions for greater risk-taking offer increased opportunities for finding female partners and, thus, for producing more offspring. For a long time, there has been selective pressure on men to maximize the acquisition of resources and to attract women. Interestingly, the authors of the study even suggest leaning towards risky investment behavior in order to accrue larger resources and to gain an advantage over other men. It seems that this is logical advice, but the conditions for taking risks are less and less favorable from year to year. Unfortunately, research on the levels of testosterone in men is somewhat puzzling.

A study on testosterone levels among approximately 1,500 men in Boston, Massachusetts indicates that blood testosterone levels in men fell drastically over the 17-year study period.[74] It's natural for the level of testosterone in every man to decrease with age; however, the average testosterone level among 60-year-olds examined from 2002 to 2004 was nearly 20% lower than the average testosterone level of 60-year-olds examined in from 1987 to 1989, and about 15% lower than that of 70-year-olds examined between 1987 and 1989. Certainly, our lifestyle has a major influence on the generational decline in testosterone. The difference in the reported health complaints from the periods 1987–1989 and 2002–2004 was 11% more cancers, 4% more diabetes, 9% more heart disease, 18% more cases of hypertension, and 19% more other reported ailments. The share of respondents who did not take any prescription drugs fell from 40% to 0%. Body weight also increased among the subjects. An interesting fact is that in the study, the number of smokers dropped from 25% to 9%, which may also be a cause of the reduced testosterone. Researchers note that among people who quit smoking, testosterone levels are typically lower.[75] Unfortunately, there was nothing on the questionnaire about the use of pornography, but given the increasingly easier access to it, it could have had an impact on the result.

In slightly more recent studies, cited by the Endocrine Society in Australia, testosterone levels studied over 5 consecutive years fell by less than 1% per year on average.[76] About 1,500 men aged 35–80 were examined (average age: 54). It was noted that the more considerable drops occurred in overweight men who quit smoking or

---

[74] Thomas G. Travison, Andre B. Araujo, Amy B. O'Donnell, Varant Kupelian, John B. McKinlay (2007): *A Population-Level Decline in Serum Testosterone Levels in American Men*.

[75] It's better to never start smoking.

[76] "Endocrine Society" (2012): *Declining testosterone levels in men not part of normal aging*.

exhibited depressive tendencies. In addition, a faster decrease in testosterone levels was also noted among the respondents who were not married. This was probably due to the limited intercourse with women, but one might also conjecture that it was due to a tendency toward pornography and solitary masturbation.

The studies described above demonstrate that our lifestyle largely affects our testosterone levels. It can even be concluded that the progress of civilization inevitably leads to a reduction in testosterone. With all this in mind, we must take exceptional care of our lifestyle and watch out for any external factors that may disturb our hormonal balance. First of all, we should remember that any sexual stimuli that are not connected with real women—or avoiding relationships with women—can lower testosterone levels and cause depressive states that also lead to reduced testosterone levels. All of this seems particularly important in the context of investment.

It's worth noting that in a study on testosterone levels and the propensity for risk, researchers studied the subjects' willingness to bet money in a very risky game (a coin toss, so only a 50% chance of winning). From the point of view of an experienced investor, taking such a risk would be frowned upon. Ultimately, you should invest and make every effort to maximize the expected return on capital. No major investment ever relies purely on luck. Another study, however, showed that a higher level of testosterone doesn't only favor the courage to take risks. In 2008, the results of a study conducted on a real trading floor in the global financial center, the City of London, were published.[77] Seventeen traders, for 8 working days, twice a day (at the beginning and end of intensive trade) had their saliva testosterone levels measured. Simultaneously, the investment results were logged. The traders who

---

[77] J. M. Coates, J. Herbert (2008): *Endogenous steroids and financial risk taking on a London trading floor*.

participated in the study were between 18 and 38 years old (average age: 27.6 years) and traded in sums from £100,000 to £100,000,000 pounds. Individual participants' average investment results from the previous month were used as a baseline. On this basis, the study days were divided into days with above-average profits and days with below-average profits or a loss. It turned out that the testosterone levels were significantly higher on the days with above-average earnings than on the days when their earnings were lower. Afterwards, the days were divided into those when the morning testosterone level was higher than the median, and those when the testosterone level was lower than the median (a difference of about 25%). This time it also turned out that the results achieved were much better on the days when the morning testosterone level was higher than the median. It is worth mentioning that the difference between the average results from high morning-testosterone-level days and the average results from low morning-testosterone-level days was colossal.

This study directly shows the positive effect of high testosterone levels on success in investments. The authors of the study emphasize that success in investment not only causes, but also results in a surge in testosterone level, which may again be conducive to success (failure does not work positively on testosterone levels, whereas variability in the results raises cortisol levels). Let me remind you that elevated testosterone endorses perseverance in one's pursuits, an appetite for risk, and the courage to face new things, that is, it brings out the qualities which are desirable among investors. Levels of testosterone which are too high or too long-lasting may also lead to unwelcome investment behavior: seeking drama, taking harmful risks, and displaying unwarranted optimism. It's worth remembering that after accomplishing something, you should give yourself a moment to cool down. The above study, however, once again shows how much hormonal economy impacts our success and how important it is to maintain a natural balance and, in particular, not to lower our testosterone levels.

7.3. A STEP INTO THE UNKNOWN

My first experiences with taking risks came in my college days, before I ever got involved in business ideas. Unfortunately, this was during the time when I was regularly visiting pornography websites. My testosterone level was low practically all the time, which made it difficult for me to control myself. Although I lived, for the most part, in a state of anxiety and my life resembled that of vegetation, I still dreamed of vast wealth. Poker tournaments and the substantial winnings of professional card players were becoming hip at my university. So, my first experience with risk took place at the college bridge club, whose members really played poker. My savings very quickly began to dry up. The better, regular players found me to be easy prey and easily put me up to betting money. I was typically in a very bad mood after every session. I wasn't able to take a risk because when I did, I couldn't keep my nerves in check. Also, when I got a better hand, my behavior gave me away. When my savings were nearly depleted, I said goodbye to the bridge club for a long time.

I saw another opportunity to earn money on the stock market. After all, two parties participate in every transaction, where one party earns and the other one loses. I was studying economics, so my chances of becoming the winning party seemed to have gone up. In hindsight, my choices of assets were surprisingly good. The problem is that the volatility of the markets and the fluctuations of the prices were paralyzing for me. Instead of creating a diversified portfolio of popular stocks and calmly waiting for them to grow, I scrutinized the stock listings and charts for days on end. My nerves were on the fritz, as I sold my stocks in reaction to every price drop, and bought them after every increase, which contradicts the basic rule: buy low, sell high. When I saw red numbers on the ticker next to my stocks, I felt a momentary surge of stress, despair, and fear that I would lose everything then and there. When the price of my stocks remained below the purchase price for over an hour, I would sell the assets, overwhelmed by my wrecked nerves. Most of the time, after a short while, the price would annoyingly return above my purchase price. When the price would start to rise and all of my enthusiasm came back, I would buy the stocks again, fearing that the price would rise and I would miss out. As it turned out, after the purchase, the potential for the price increase was usually exhausted and it would all start all over again.

Why do I think that my decisions regarding stock picks were good? Because I chose healthy companies with high growth potential. This was a textbook choice, yet the effects of organic growth of the companies' value could only be noticed after a while. The problem was that, for some reason, I expected immediate profits. Going against everything that would be advisable, I impatiently inspected the daily charts and price changes, without any idea about the technical analysis. This jumble of thoughts and nerves lasted for a few weeks and when my savings once again dipped to an alarming level, I abandoned my adventure with the stock market. Then, of course, I blamed the entire market—the stock market is manipulated and the big players dictate the conditions—but I couldn't see my lamentable behavior for what it was.

It's only now, a few years later, that I can see I was losing the battle of the capital market with myself, way before I even entered the stock exchange game. My body was weak, I was susceptible to emotions, and my nerves and stress prevented me from keeping a clear head. My habits, based on quick and easy pleasures, would not allow me to get accustomed to unstable situations. In addition, my hormonal balance—strained by frequent pornography viewing and masturbation—prevented me from feeling confident. I still felt an unreasonable fear which was amplified by any risk, even the slightest one. Even going out to a party at night or taking the bus seemed scary to me. Any situation in which I had no influence on the surrounding reality was a source of fear. This may seem inconceivable and my behavior and observations may have suggested paranoia, but that's how the male body can feel when its hormonal economy is disturbed. It is exactly the same feeling as that experienced by men who are quitting anabolic steroids, drugs which drastically upset the endocrine system. Very often, after a man takes steroids, his organs are no longer able to maintain the appropriate level of testosterone and other hormones. Putting aside the way in which such activities affect a man's hormonal balance, there is no doubt that all practices causing a hormonal imbalance can have dire consequences for the body. It was only after a few months of abandoning pornography and masturbation that I stopped experiencing the anxiety that had previously accompanied me. My guess is that only then did my hormone economy return to a state of equilibrium. At the same time, I changed my lifestyle and became a more active person; I started to spend more time with people, to get dates with women, and to play sports. Only then came the time when I started to take justifiable risks.

Having worked for some time as an investment banking analyst, I learned a lot about capital markets and the behavior of major investors. My superiors—Jack and the director, Frank—focused exclusively on core business (the mergers and acquisitions department, to be precise, which was also associated with considerable income), while almost all the other analysts were proponents of actively participating in capital market trading. Taking advantage of the fact that our bank most often dealt with small enterprises and rarely with publicly listed businesses, employees could freely invest in an almost unlimited number of different assets. This didn't present a conflict of interest. Initially, I was skeptical about my colleagues playing on the stock market. I could still remember my own adventure with the stock exchange and the money I lost on it. Still, as I didn't want to isolate myself from my coworkers, I had to participate in daily debates about the stock market. Slowly, month after month, I became more and more involved in the conversations, allowing myself to express bolder and bolder forecasts of stock prices and of economic variables. A very important perk of our job was the daily briefing of business news, thanks to which, I gained valuable insight into the markets after a few months. I tried not to mince words, but to verify my theses. On the market, we encountered new situations every day, which also became the subject of debates. For example, we discussed elections around the world—who would win and how the markets would behave in specific cases. We discussed spectacular mergers and acquisitions, stock exchange debuts, etc. We exchanged insights and in the case of conflicting opinions, we listened to each other's arguments. Eventually, each argument was verified by the market. Right now, I am very grateful for the time we spent at breakfast, during breaks and afternoons, debating the markets. Thanks to this, we learned much more than at college. Working in investment banking was very instructive, but being around the people who worked there was even more educational.

It is important to try to spend every day with people you can learn from. Interestingly, you can learn even more by arguing with them. Over time, it turned out that my forecasts were often accurate, and standing by and watching the markets was no longer enough for me. At that time, a popular technological company decided to offer shares on the stock exchange. We had long argued with the analysts about the wisdom of buying stocks in an IPO.[78]

---

[78] IPO (Initial Public Offering) – when a company or it's owners sell shares on the stock market for the first time

We all agreed that the company's profits were embarrassing and that the long-term plans of the owner were rather doubtful. I was the only one who thought that the interest in this particular company going public was so strong that it would hike up the stock price on the day it debuts. I signed up for the IPO and a few years after my first infamous adventure with the stock exchange, I actively returned to capital market trading. My colleagues were surprised that I was taking such a risky step, but my rational mind wouldn't allow me to miss the chance. I committed about half of my savings in the IPO with the strong resolution to sell all my stock on the first day of trading. As I was at work during the debut and I had to perform my duties before the listings started rolling in, I set two automatic sell orders: to sell when the price falls below 15% and to sell when the price rises above 30%. I also decided that if, by the end of the day, the price was still within this range, I would sell the stocks at the current price. I admit that the whole day I was thinking about my stocks and that I glanced at the trading indexes from time to time despite my responsibilities. I was tempted to close my position, because in the morning I noticed that the trading volume and price volatility were high. Then I remembered that I had come to terms with the possibility of failure and that in the event of a mishap, the stop loss order[79] would close my positions.

That day, as usual, I had a lot of work to do. We were closing an important transaction and had to supervise the flow of important documents. I didn't pay attention to the stock listings for a few hours and when at some point I looked at my brokerage account, the position was closed. It turned out that when the shares debuted, the price increased by about 40%, while my take profit order[80] closed the

---

[79] An order to sell stocks when the price *falls below* the indicated level.

[80] An order to sell stocks when the price *rises above* the indicated level.

position at 30%. From one day to the next, I became several thousand dollars richer. It was a wonderful feeling, but with all my strength I tried not to show my elation in front of my coworkers. Suppressing my euphoria also helped me to control the excitement and to use common sense, because after such a success on the stock market, it's easy to let one's guard down.

I believe that a solid analysis of the situation had a big impact on this success, but what mattered even more was making the right—rather courageous—decision. Apart from the job interview negotiations at the bank, during which I took a risk, it was my first serious risk-taking effort that involved a relatively large portion of my resources. After that, I began to consider investment decisions and take financial risks more often. After a few months, I had already built an asset portfolio based on my strategy. In that portfolio, I always had stocks of two to five promising companies with solid foundations for growth. The second part of my portfolio—the much smaller one—was cash at hand, which I invested in short-term risky transactions based on one-off events, such as stock exchange debuts in China, trade in emerging market indexes, or a short sale of declining businesses. This second part of the portfolio didn't always provide an income, but when it did, I moved the profit to my investments in solid companies. Mostly, I avoided financial leverage, but sometimes in what I considered to be obvious wins, I couldn't resist the temptation. In this way, my funds grew year by year at a strong rate. According to the textbook approach to investing, my strategy was classified as a high-risk strategy. However, over time I simply learned to take risks and the losses didn't have any effect on me. I just made a mistake in my assumptions, I figured, so I would always scrupulously note that mistake the following day and take it into account in subsequent investments.

At some point, I began to feel comfortable taking risks, but I must also point out that my knowledge about markets and investing was growing from month to month. My salary in the bank had also improved, so my self-confidence about the funds I was investing also grew. Maintaining a healthy lifestyle and getting rid of self-destructive habits also helped me to regain my sense of self-worth. If it hadn't been for escaping pornography and masturbation, I wouldn't have forced myself to set ambitious plans, I wouldn't have given myself a chance to tackle such a complex field, and I still would have been shy—for example, I would have been afraid to enter into debates with my coworkers and to take risks. My hormone economy finally allowed me to feel strong. The people in my life began to take me seriously; my bosses respected my opinion, and I also started getting attention from women. Don't get me wrong: by investing in the markets, I didn't make a fortune, but I significantly improved my standard of living, and I transferred my risk-taking skills to other areas. I started to travel, I got involved in a serious relationship, I met a lot of new people. Despite living mainly in cities without access to the sea, I could afford to learn to surf and to travel the world in search of the right waves. I began to live a full life and to enjoy the most beautiful things in life. All because I became accustomed to the risk that I had previously avoided like the plague.

At the start, risk taking is like breaking in a wild horse: you never know what its next move will be. However, you can tame this wild horse into a farm animal. Unfortunately, without taking risks, it will be very difficult to achieve above-average goals, so you must learn to do it and to feel comfortable with it. This requires a bit of courage, but you can minimize the uncertainty and unpredictability. Risk is taken to achieve benefits, so it is important to minimize it to zero, that is, to be informed and to try to predict how things might go and how far you can venture into the unknown. Remember that taking risk without knowing its scope or consciously taking a very high risk is gambling. I strongly advise against it.

When a rodeo cowboy gets on a horse, he is determined to stay on its back for as long as possible. If he wants to win, he can't get scared and jump off. If you take up a challenge, you can't back down until you've met all your goals. You need to be resistant to the horse's unexpected movements. It takes a lot of perseverance, strength, and self-control to stay on its back. This attempt to ride a wild horse may represent starting a business or buying a house, but huge cultural and social projects as well. On your way to completing the challenge, there will be a lot of temptations to retreat, temptations heightened by fear of failure. It's necessary to persist in your endeavor and to have the mental strength to go along with it, which is certainly easier to achieve with a stable hormonal economy and overall balance of the body. Of course, if we have no doubt that our decision is wrong, we must withdraw from it. However, if our doubts arise only from fear, then we must remain firm. From my own experience, I know that it is better to lose because of incorrect assumptions and to learn from this experience than to lose or not gain enough when the assumptions were right. A missed opportunity hurts much more than a misidentified opportunity.

All major challenges require knowledge, and investments in capital markets require financial knowledge and experience. I advise against investing by guesstimating and through buying assets blindly because this is nothing more than gambling. Large architectural projects require knowledge about construction and adherence to safety standards. All social programs have to be thought over and analyzed in terms of whether they will bring more harm than good. For example, it should be assessed whether the recipients need financial support or rather access to education, which would create an opportunity for them to earn a living in the future. I urge you to acquire knowledge and experience: in my case, it was theory about finance and practice in the industry. When you feel confident with all the data and information you have acquired, you will know when the time is right for action. For example, you will know that it is not you who chooses the best time to invest, but that the investment opportunity comes knocking on your door. If it's possible to minimize the risk, always do so. A real man ventures into the unknown, but he does so responsibly. Risk-taking also consists of the ability to deal with failure and loss. Therefore, I encourage you to learn to take risks gradually. When you learn to do this, you'll find out that not taking a risk is often a waste. Certainly, a man's natural predisposition can facilitate this. Women are much less interested in taking risks, which is natural for them. This can be seen, for example, in the marginal numbers of women among investors on capital markets. It's probably a matter of common sense, but probably also because of the much lower levels of testosterone. Appreciate the fact that you have the opportunity to use natural doping—that is to say, testosterone—and respect it. It's not worth compromising your natural abilities with false pleasure in the form of pornography and masturbation.

8. PATIENCE IS A VIRTUE

He that can have patience can have what he will.

- Benjamin Franklin

8.1. NOTHING HAPPENS BY CHANCE

Patience plays a huge role in life—in my life as well, where patience was of particular importance in the previously described situations: the creative process and the search for ideas, self-control, negotiating, and risk-taking. Unfortunately, a propensity for quick pleasure, such as masturbating to pornography, is not conducive to patience. A man accustomed to finding pleasure at the tap of a screen will find it difficult to wait for something in the name of a long-term, much greater benefit. It will be difficult for him to give up the quick dopamine hits provided by pornography and masturbation and other drugs. Don't get me wrong, I don't mean procrastination—because you often have to act quickly—and I don't mean waiting for things that may never happen, either. I mean waiting for things that are quite sure to happen and for which patience is usually rewarded. In my case, it was learning, gathering experience, waiting for investments to bring in returns, waiting for a good business opportunity, and building a healthy relationship and mutual trust. I also patiently waited for my relinquishment of pornography and masturbation to finally pay off.

I have found that by waiting patiently and working persistently, one can achieve a real, happy life which doesn't require any aids. Waking up every day next to a loving partner, being aware of my financial security, creating a home which is a haven of peace and safety, and feeling the satisfaction derived from helping others every day provide me with a constant level of dopamine, equivalent to a joy of living that I had never before been able to maintain without destabilizing my reward system. Even small doses of dopamine for a balanced reward system are just as strong or stronger than the very high doses of dopamine for a heavily overused reward system. An example is people who abuse cocaine and other drugs, who often almost completely destroy their reward system. When the reward system is bombarded and besieged with extreme doses of dopamine over long periods of time, it can't recover for a long time. It is unable to provide any joy in life, which unfortunately often results in depression. What's worse, people are often unable to withstand the regeneration of the reward system and they return to their addictions. A very similar mechanism applies to people watching pornography.[81] It also abuses the reward system, which leads to low sensitivity to everyday sources of joy. Then you need to compensate for long-lasting states of depression with another session of pornography and masturbation. To rebuild the natural balance of the reward system, these strong stimuli must be discontinued. Self-control is necessary to resist the temptation to return to bad habits, but patience is almost equally important. The return of the reward system to its natural balance takes time. Everyone is different and for every pornography watcher, it has a different impact on the reward system, so the time needed to return to balance will be different. Different people are more or less sensitive as well, which means that not everyone will notice the return to a natural balance. I assure you, however, that when you manage to stabilize your system, your life will change for the better. From my own experience, I know that a naturally stabilized reward system is a valuable reward worth waiting for. I also had to wait for the abandonment of pornography and masturbation to bring me rewards.

When I decided to give up the sexual stimuli that were destructive for my body—pornography and masturbation—a few months or even more than a year passed before my reward system became fully restored. Once it stabilized, I began to experience even the smallest doses of dopamine and, crucially, to simply feel good all the time. It is not an urban legend that putting an end to masturbating to pornography improves your thinking and deduction skills. Thanks to this, you feel more motivated, which facilitates a heightened mental performance. Similarly, small doses of dopamine are delivered to our brain when we spend time with our loved ones, meet new people, and are nice to others and give them joy. This is also one of the reasons

---

[81] Mattebo M, Tyden T, Häggström-Nordin E, Nillson KW (2014): *Pornography consumption, psychosomatic health and depressive symptoms among Swedish adolescents.*

why people who regularly watch pornography become selfish and often cannot function in society without insincerity and insecurities.[82,83] The happiness gained through selfless contact with people is imperceptible for them.

Since my body has been in equilibrium and I get limitless benefits from it, it doesn't even occur to me to visit porn websites. I don't even pay attention to the commercialization of the naked female form in advertisements with stark-naked women. When I pass sexy women on the street, I don't ogle them. I am perfectly aware of how devoting too much of my attention to these stimuli will end for me. Thanks to the fact that my body has returned to its hormonal equilibrium, I have become even more patient than before. This is another valuable reward for my quitting pornography and masturbation.

It would seem that becoming a man and developing a manly, firm attitude is a natural consequence of puberty. Unfortunately, getting trapped in pornography use may delay this process. Patience is one feature of an exemplary frame of mind for a mature man. The other features include courage, compassion, respect for others, loyalty, honesty, honor, prudence, grace, forgiveness, humility, authenticity, self-improvement, kindness, gratitude, commitment, perseverance, tact, generosity, empathy, contentment, assertiveness, cooperation, adaptability, and righteousness. All of these qualities help in the pursuit of a prosperous and happy life. Developing them becomes much easier if the reward system and the endocrine system are in balance. A lack of patience often makes us choose shortcuts, meaning

---

[82] Kasper TE, Short MB, Milam AC (2015): *Narcissism and Internet pornography use.*

[83] Leppink EW, Chamberlain SR, Redden SA, Grant JE: *Problematic sexual behavior in young adults: Associations across clinical, behavioral, and neurocognitive variables.*

that many of these qualities are given a lower profile. As a result, our life—despite some momentary pleasures—becomes bitter and unattractive. Personally, in spite of having given up these temporary pleasures, I am still working hard on myself to acquire and refine all these qualities. However, in large part they come naturally for me. It's a very nice feeling to know that day by day, by working on myself, I am becoming a better and better person.

It's hard to believe how much depends on one's attitude, approach to life, and even one's mood. Since my life has changed, people are more willing to spend time with me, to trust me, and to cooperate with me. This is something that helps me in business and makes business easier for me. Being my new, non-pornography-watching self, I have discovered my true skills and potential. I've stopped seeing steep hills and winding paths ahead of me, and have started to see an ocean of possibilities instead.

8.2. RESEARCH ON PATIENCE

In the 1960s and 1970s at Stanford University, psychologist Walter Mischel conducted a series of experiments exploring the issue of choosing more gratification available in the future over smaller pleasures which are available immediately. One of the experiments was popularized under the name "the marshmallow test". The children in the study could decide whether they wanted to receive a prize in the form of a snack right away, or a doubled snack after waiting for a short time. The children themselves chose the snack that they would receive as a reward. Most often it was their favorite dessert—marshmallows, cookies, or candy. The researcher informed each child about their options, then left the snack in front of him or her and left the room for about 15 minutes. In this way, he tested whether the children would resist the temptation and be willing to wait for a bigger reward.

Out of the 600 children who took part in the study, the majority of them tried to wait in the name of increased profits, but only about one-third of those who tried managed to receive a larger snack. The children who did this helped themselves by covering their eyes or turning away from the source of temptation. Some of them released their tension by kicking at the table or pulling at their braids. More than 10 years after the experience, questionnaires were sent to parents of the children who had participated in the study. The parents of those children who were able to delay gratification long enough to get a greater reward described their now-adolescent children as more capable than their peers. These children also caused fewer problems at home, dealt with stress more capably, and had no trouble with concentration, with attention span, or with maintaining friendships. Notably, the children who were able to restrain themselves in order to receive a larger future gratification achieved much higher results on the standardized SAT.

The marshmallow test shows that patience largely determines our success in life. In an earlier study, Mischel showed that this ability is not genetically or ethnically determined. Whether we will be patient or not depends on whether we are conscious of the benefits of waiting and how much we can control ourselves. As I have mentioned, we can practice self-control, so our patience can grow. It is good news that we can become more and more persistent and thus increase our chances of success. But can we also damage our patience?

Some researchers decided to study what influence pornography use has on a person's patience, specifically the ability to postpone gratification over time in the name of higher profits.[84] In the first step, the volunteers were

---

[84] Negash S, Sheppard NV, Lambert NM, Fincham FD (2016): *Trading Later Rewards for Current Pleasure: Pornography Consumption and Delay Discounting*.

asked how often they watched pornography, then the researchers checked their willingness to choose a bigger reward available later in time instead of a small reward available immediately. The dependence was unilateral: the more often the subject watched pornography, the less attractive the deferred larger reward seemed to them. A second study checked whether abstaining from pornography for three weeks would improve the skill of postponing gratification. Subjects in the control group refrained from their favorite food group for three weeks, while not giving up pornography. The test results confirmed the hypothesis. The group who stopped watching pornography for three weeks showed a greater ability to postpone gratification, with both groups achieving similar results before the start of the experiment. Both groups practiced self-control during the abstinence period, so if the ability to put off gratification in time improved due to better self-control, abstinence from pornography honed this ability much more. A similar result was obtained in a study of over 2,000 pornography users, in which a longer time of abstinence increased the capability of the participants to delay gratification.[85] This is more proof that withdrawal from pornography use significantly enhances a person's desirable traits, trains them in self-control, and increases their chances of success in life.

The above-mentioned studies demonstrate that watching pornography has a destructive effect on our patience. The constant search for pleasure, typical for pornography users, leads to increased impulsiveness.[86,87] It also involves

---

[85] (2016): *How Abstinence Affects Preferences.*

[86] EW Leppink, SR Chamberlain, SA Redden, JE Grant
(2016):*Problematic sexual behavior in young adults: Associations across clinical, behavioral, and neurocognitive variables.*

[87] Messina B, Fuentes D, Tavares H, Abdo CH, Scanavino MT (2017):
Executive Functioning of Sexually Compulsive and Non-Sexually Compulsive Men Before and After Watching an Erotic Video.

physical changes in those parts of the brain which are responsible for patience.[88] Importantly, the deterioration of the ability to defer pleasure over time also applies to those who rarely watch pornography. In summary, patience does not depend on one's genes or individual predispositions, but on one's everyday behavior.

8.3. THE FRUITS OF MY LABOR

My first adventures with business and the stock market ended in disaster. This was mainly because my frame of mind was weak, I didn't apply myself to it and I expected immediate profits. It took me a long time before I learned that earning money requires an idea, mature knowledge, and time. Even when I was trading in shoes and clothes over the Internet, I realized that you can't speed up the pace by overstocking too much or hastening the sales with prices that are too low. I waited calmly until my stock slowly sold out and, in the meantime, I would look for opportunities to buy goods at attractive prices. I adopted a similar strategy after completely quitting pornography and with my first major investments. Despite my tremendous excitement, I didn't rush that either. I didn't throw my money at the market without thinking it through. Even when I found the desired asset, I adeptly waited for the price to drop so I could purchase it as cheaply as possible. It's true that sometimes it only takes a few moments to increase your capital on the stock market, but the entire decision-making process and the preparation for the transaction take much more time. I also learned to live with the awareness that I was risking my savings. Previously, I was unable to focus on other matters when I knew that the value of my assets was constantly fluctuating. In the past, every new business

---

[88] Kacey Ballard, Brian Knutson (2009): *Dissociable neural representations of future reward magnitude and delay during temporal discounting*.

idea seemed like a golden opportunity and I was ready to hastily, without deeper analysis, invest my funds. Then I would tremble with horror ("What on earth have I done?"). Only with time did I notice that there are plenty of ideas. There's no need to hurry, the right one will eventually come along. That was the case with the first major business in which I became involved.

My attitude began to change, and more and more people with similar interests appeared around me. They trusted me, shared ideas with me and offered me their commitment. I know from experience that you should talk about your ideas, but only with experienced and knowledgeable people who will be able to give you valuable tips. I used to talk about my plans in the past and wait for advice from people who had no clue. That was a mistake. Most often, this ended in seeking confirmation from the other person or even suggesting the answers myself, or worse—getting some bad advice. These are the effects of setting up a business without the proper knowledge and with an unstable hormone economy and a broken reward system.

With time, I became the person who people asked for advice about their businesses. After all, while working in investment banking and learning the ropes investing on the stock market, learning about markets and industries, I learned a great deal. My self-confidence and the calm that emanated from me were of great importance. After a year or so of not masturbating to pornography, my reward system and endocrine system had reached a balance, which allowed me to effectively build the desired attitude. My friends from college, usually very ambitious people, had avoided me because they considered me a lazy hustler, and a rash, untrustworthy guy. My weak body betrayed an unstable demeanor, which was fearful and full of doubt. Now everyone began to change their minds and the longer I spent with them, the more they gained trust in me. I was friendly, enthusiastic, and forgiving, but not too intrusive. I had a lot of empathy and openness, thanks to which I interpreted human emotions and gestures very well. Formerly, friends distanced themselves from me and didn't like hanging out with me. Afterwards, they often invited me to parties, arranged to have lunch together, and wanted to hear my opinion on various topics. They often came to me with interesting business ideas, asking for advice or encouraging me to get involved. Many of these ideas were good, but I felt that it was better to wait for something which I saw as a great opportunity. At some point, I began to value my energy highly, so it seemed a shame to waste it on labor-intensive projects with a doubtful future. Honestly, I really liked the people around me; I liked myself and how I behaved toward others. I could politely refuse them, and what's more, give them valuable tips.

    I was waiting for an idea that would be a smash hit. Finally, an opportunity presented itself. One day, near my bank, I ran into Kevin, an acquaintance who I met while working in auditing. It was thanks to him that a few years earlier they didn't fire me, so I couldn't resist and invited him for lunch. We began to catch up and, one thing leading to another, it turned out that we think the same way. Kevin had worked much longer in auditing than me, but when he left the well-known Big 4 company, he didn't look for another job. He had a lot of expertise in environmental protection laws, so, along with a few friends, he set up a consulting company. They knew how to save manufacturing companies millions of dollars on tax breaks by implementing the appropriate environmental procedures. Why did Kevin tell me about all this? Although his company was doing a great job, his clients refused to pay them much. Entrepreneurs were often skeptical about environmental protection, with fears about efficiency and higher costs. Often, they were doubtful that even if commissioning Kevin's company would produce results, it wouldn't bring them any profits. Interestingly, Kevin claimed that thanks to his service, 90% of the companies saw savings of several million dollars in the first year, while 10% of them broke even on the costs incurred.

Kevin was happy that he could run the company, but he was still looking for a way to boost his income. He simply didn't have the experience and the knowledge that would help him do it. When he worked in auditing, his manager or partner would sell an audit service for a specific price, usually depending on the turnover of the audited firm. His auditing firm also often placed bids for tenders where several similar companies were usually competing for the contracts by offering lower prices. Kevin and his associates tried to price their services the same way—by estimating the amount of time required and adding a standard profit margin. However, he didn't take into account the fact that auditing services were compulsory for many businesses: they had to have their financial statements inspected at least once a year. Although Kevin's service might have seemed attractive, the entrepreneurs were not obliged to use it and they readily bargained for better prices. When their attempts failed, they simply didn't express any further interest. Kevin didn't know very much about business relationships. He hadn't participated in the talks between the auditing firm partners and their clients. He didn't have the opportunity to see what sales at this level look like. What's worse, after so many years spent in the auditing industry, he didn't have many serious business contacts. He only knew other auditors or accountants from the companies they audited. He sold his services using so-called "guerilla tactics," by calling from the street and begging secretaries for the phone numbers to important people or by spamming people's inboxes with advertisements. Occasionally, a friendly accountant would fix him up with the president of their company. It was also rare that a satisfied customer recommended his company to their contacts.

When I heard his story, I knew almost immediately how to help Kevin. I told him straightforwardly, "I will increase your company's revenue tenfold in return for 40% of the shares." Kevin looked at me in disbelief at first, but decided to listen to what I had to say. Well, the first thing I could offer him was hundreds of contacts that I had amassed while working in a bank. In contrast to the auditing industry, the services of investment banking were always carried out in close consultation with the owners of the companies—our clients. As I wrote before, after a few months of work, I had already taken part in talks with investors and presidents, and after only a few years I was managing projects myself, sometimes availing myself of the knowledge of my superiors. I had such a commanding manner that I often earned the trust of some serious businessmen.

The second thing that I could bring to Kevin's business was a new way of settling accounts with clients. The bank in which I worked most often settled up with clients by way of a monthly retainer—a fixed, relatively low fee—and what's known as the success fee, which is a negotiated percentage of the transaction we conducted, and it was a substantial part of our income. The retainer covered our labor and office space costs, while the success fee generated massive amounts of money, which allowed my bosses to live in expensive apartments and to drive luxury cars. So I advised Kevin to lower the fixed fee for his services to a minimum, or to scrap it completely, and to have the main compensation depend on the profits resulting from services rendered in the first year, preferably 10–30%, depending on the success of the negotiations. In the end, 90% of the projects were effective. Kevin agreed to working with me before even finishing his lunch. At first, he didn't want to agree to me receiving such a large share of the company. Apart from him, three other people also owned the firm, so their share would shrink from 25% to 15%. I said that I understood his hesitancy, but I assured him that the company's turnover would be 10 times higher, so for them it would be a six-fold increase. In addition, I pledged that if the revenues didn't rise above a certain threshold, I would completely hand back my share of the profit. That was the argument I convinced Kevin with.

He still got indignant for a moment when I said that I wouldn't work in his company on a daily basis. I couldn't quit my job at the bank because I would lose the source of new clients for Kevin. Truth be told, even then I had such a broad base of contacts in business that I wouldn't have been able to approach them all in half a year, and Kevin and his three partners were able to process at most one project a month. However, I liked my job, I was still young, and the experience I was gaining in my job at the bank was invaluable. I also dreamed about having my own business, and by keeping my job, I could gather the relevant knowledge and stumble across the right opportunity. What's more, as a bank employee I had a broad overview of the capital markets all the time, which was also difficult for me to give up. After all, I was constantly reinvesting my money into securities. My last condition for Kevin was that I would have first dibs in talking and negotiating with the client I am trying to win. This gave me the chance to strengthen my relationships with businesspeople and to practice my soft skills, including negotiating skills. After agreeing on all the terms, we signed the necessary agreements, after which I gained a 40% stake in Kevin's consulting company.

After we got through all the paperwork, I almost immediately started acquiring clients. It turned out that I didn't have to do much more work in the process. I was carrying out my duties in the bank while making appointments with the entrepreneurs I knew. Within the first few weeks of working with Kevin, I had procured contracts for our company for the next quarter. The businesspeople agreed to my terms because they didn't bear very much risk. There was nothing left to do but expand the consulting company and employ more consultants. Serious revenue began to accrue after a year, because we had to wait for the effects of our services. Still, waiting for this profit paid off.

You may have assumed that the business with which I identified my success and which is partly responsible for the "Get Rich" part of this book's title would be spectacular. You might have anticipated that this business would be associated with new technologies, the Internet, and all the start-up madness that the media attack us with every day. Yes, I also hoped that I would be one of those dazzling young minds to come up with a surprisingly simple idea and win over millions of consumers around the world. It hasn't happened yet. I am still waiting for my dream business and am trying to give myself as many opportunities as possible to find it. I'm developing my ventures. I also seize all other opportunities that bring me closer to wealth. By working at the bank, running a company with Kevin, and investing in securities, I have gained financial security, priceless experience, and a lot of acquaintances. All of this will certainly make it easier for me to reach my desired goal. I'm not worried if I will ever see my business idea materialize, because opportunities will always arise.

The most important thing is that at that time I felt how much my attitude to life and my mood differed from a few years before, when I used to spend a lot of time watching pornography and masturbating. It was then that I realized how much had changed in my life since I had given up these artificial stimuli. I had the impression that these stimuli caused a lot of harm to my body and mind. I couldn't just waive all of this aside and forget about it: I started researching far and wide to find out how artificial stimuli affected such important matters so destructively. The change that occurred in me concerned my self-confidence, self-control, courage, patience, my ability to talk with people, the way I treated women, negotiating skills, risk-taking, ability to learn, and mental performance. Fear, laziness, malaise, and problems with my reproductive system disappeared. This was too much to let the subject pass by in silence. That was when I came up with the idea of writing this book.

9. REAL PEOPLE

Strive not to be a success, but rather to be of value.

- Albert Einstein

9.1. BUILDING RELATIONSHIPS

Because of pornography, we may objectify people. Women can become merely providers of sexual sensations. The abuse of sexual stimuli can also impact our friendships and acquaintances. There is a risk of our relationships becoming shallow, of us choosing a friendship only to suit our own needs, such as material gain or entertainment.

Because of pornography, we become self-centered; the people around us sooner or later realize this and it becomes difficult for us to maintain our existing relationships and to build new ones. Pornography can also make us feel worthless, make us withdraw into ourselves and to isolate ourselves from society. We may behave unnaturally among people, feeling insecure and seeing dark conspiracies everywhere we look. Also, difficulty making eye contact while talking with others is a typical problem for porn users.

Everyday relationships with people—especially mutual kindness, empathy, and friendship—create a series of chemical reactions in the body. They provide oxytocin, among other things, thanks to which we should enjoy these relationships. Once again, if we abuse the reward system too much—by watching pornography, for example—then ordinary dealings with people will not bring us any satisfaction or joy, but we will start treating them like a tedious chore. A study of over 2,000 users of pornography showed that abstinence caused increased altruism, more extroverted behavior, increased conscientiousness, and decreased neuroticism.

Perhaps you think that not everyone needs the company of others and that some can manage perfectly well without it. However, the truth is that most often in business as in many other undertakings, knowledge and the ability to win people over are essential. It is precisely when we spend time with people and try to be the best we can for them that we practice such skills. If we don't spend time with others, don't broaden our circle of friends, and don't start to feel comfortable around people, then we won't learn to interact with them and we won't be able to cope in various situations. The business world is diverse and requires the ability to adapt to changing conditions. In business, there are often talks with people from different cultures, with different customs, and with different moral values, so the ability to interact with people from various backgrounds, being a good judge of character—or in other words, social intelligence—are invaluable assets. The ability to conduct an open discussion and to come to an agreement, often with a complete stranger, makes business much easier. It is our gestures, words, and facial expressions that hold the key to winning over the other person; it is also his or her gestures, words, and facial expressions, though, which betray his or her thoughts, and only by being able to communicate and to interpret his or her reactions will we be able to decipher these thoughts. Also, not everyone will be friendly to us and we will often have to persuade people to give us the information we need, for example. By being able to steer the conversation, bringing up the relevant subjects at the right moment, we can start a discussion on the topics that matter to us.

Patience is important in the art of conversation. Good communicators know that sometimes it is better to wait for a more opportune moment to talk than to raise an important subject at the wrong moment. Those who watch porn can become impatient and, therefore, are unable to have successful conversations. Very rarely in business do we get a satisfactory answer when we ask straightforwardly about an issue that we care about, unless it is something trivial or the interests of the other person are served by answering us. In business, it is usually the case that if the other party notices your interest in a particular matter, they immediately ascribe a higher value to information about it and will reluctantly divulge that information for free. They might, for example, expect equally valuable information in return. Someone may also try to extract information from us, so we must also be vigilant about what and to whom we reveal what we know. Also, we don't always get a client or supplier with good intentions, and thanks to our experience interacting with people we will have a better chance of discerning his or her real motives.

Another important issue in business is having extensive contacts and acquaintances. It is thanks to them that we can get access to important people or consult someone on things which are over our heads. Friendships and contacts allow you to obtain information from the market that is not available through official channels. These acquaintances can help to broaden your knowledge, to connect many links into a functioning business, or to acquire lucrative commissions. In most cases, it was an acquaintance who opened a door to prosperity, so having a wide range of contacts and valuable friends is often half the battle. By interacting with people and gaining experience with relationships, we will be more and more effective in obtaining precious knowledge and useful contacts. However, we must be honest, sincere, helpful, and—above all else—selfless and disinterested. This might seem to be a contradiction, but the benefits of knowing somebody are meant to be a potential result, not a cause. We must behave in such a way as to become valuable for others in order for them to want to be our friends. Such behavior will certainly be met with approval and will pay off at the right time.

The ability to interact with people is mainly profitable in sales. To a large extent, sales determine the success of a business and only thanks to sales do businesses function and earn profits. I will skip over the stages of identifying market trends and inventing and delivering the product, though having people skills helps in these areas as well. If you are talking to a potential buyer and sensing his or her needs and reactions, the sale becomes much easier. It's true that there are several proven strategies of effective sales that work on the majority of ordinary people, but even in this case, it's necessary to correctly interpret the buyer's behavior and to take appropriate action at the right time. Memorizing the rules alone will not produce such results as social intelligence. Even if we are selling products over the Internet, we need to know which channels to use to reach the consumer and what slogans will convince him or her to buy our goods. In the case of major transactions, social intelligence and the ability to put your best foot forward will ensure success. Only by hanging out with people, talking to them, solving problems, or even arguing and seeking agreement, will we practice social intelligence—something irreplaceable in business. Even in the case of corporate employees, higher rungs on the corporate ladder often involve the sale of the company's services or products. When working in the marketing department of an electronics manufacturer, in fast-moving consumer goods (FMCG), business services, consulting or investment banking, we finally live to see the moment when we have to land a significant client and win a huge project for the company. If we are serious about business, then we have to reckon with the need to master the ability to sell: product sales, services, the company itself, or even to sell ourselves.

Masturbating to pornography is not conducive to building relationships. Most often, it causes a severe reduction in self-esteem and self-confidence, which the people around us can easily pick up on. When we feel insecure, we adopt a defensive stance, we unknowingly unmask our weaknesses, and often give the impression of insincerity. Such an attitude may even arouse suspicion in the person we are talking to. Because of our weakened empathy and feeble enthusiasm, even when we have the best intentions the other person may interpret our motives as plotting and scheming. During the conversation, it is important to show understanding and a genuine interest in the other person. The ability to look them in the eyes is also imperative. Only when we do this are we entitled to address essential issues. You can now see how much we lose by giving up ordinary relationships with people around us. Maintaining good relationships is an invaluable practice that can be used on the path to success. By replacing these relationships with pornography and solitude, we miss our chance to grow and we turn our path to success into a real struggle.

9.2. JUMPING IN AT THE DEEP END

When I became a shareholder in Kevin's consulting company, it became my responsibility to sell his services. Although I knew a lot of entrepreneurs—potential clients—I had never done business with them personally. I always acted as an analyst or adviser, and it was my bosses, Jack and Frank, who endorsed the services of the investment bank with their faces. My job was to be reliable in any matter regarding the transactions, but I hadn't dealt with sales yet. On the other hand, my attitude and responsibility won me the trust of significant clients. I also knew a certain group of entrepreneurs with whom I was on a first-name basis. During the projects we often ate lunch together and at the table we discussed topics not only related to the project. Sometimes, presidents of companies even introduced me to their daughters, suggesting that I was a good candidate for son-in-law. I decided to sell Kevin's services starting with them. I decided that it was better not to plan sales strategies too much. I was afraid that I might behave unnaturally in front of these clients who had a good opinion of me.

I made my first phone call to Mr. Anders, a conservative businessman from the agricultural sector, for whom we had carried out the acquisition of a rival firm. When he answered the phone, he was a bit surprised that I was calling, but after a moment he asked how I was doing and how our bank was doing. I told him a bit about the market and passed on some business news which couldn't be obtained from official sources and which interested him, and then I revealed the actual reason for my phone call. Again, he was surprised by my words, but he agreed to a brief meeting during which I could tell him more about our service. When I arrived at his office a few days later, I found him in a rather unfriendly mood. First, he asked if my superiors at the bank knew what I was doing. Jack and Frank didn't realize that I was running my own business while also working for them. I replied that there was no conflict of interest and that if my bosses considered my additional business to conflict with my work for the bank, I would choose the consulting company over the bank. Mr. Anders reprimanded me. He stated that he highly values the loyalty of his employees and would not approve of them having a side business. He caught me off guard with these words, but I didn't give up. I had to use my five minutes. Mr. Anders spared me his time, even though he was a very busy man. I thanked him politely for his remark and said that he was right. Then I went into the history of Kevin's business and explained in detail what the service entailed. I enumerated all of the potential benefits and I pointed out how low-risk it is. I presented to him the people who are in charge of carrying out the service and their experience. I also quoted some client testimonials and gave some examples where the services had proved to be particularly fruitful. At the end, I promised to inform my superiors at the bank about what I do in my spare time. Mr. Anders was intrigued by the story I told him, though he tried not to show it. He said he would consider my offer, and said goodbye in a cold tone of voice. After leaving his office, I felt that I had achieved a small victory. Although I hadn't yet sold the service, I was proud of my attitude and of how I had conducted the conversation. I also knew that Mr. Anders really needed the service I was selling him at that time and that he was a rational person. I was not wrong. After a few days, his secretary called me and asked for a draft of a contract.

Just like I had promised Mr. Anders, I went to Frank and told him about my shares in Kevin's company and described my role in his business. Frank listened in astonishment and with interest, but he did not show approval. I explained to him that there was no conflict of interest in my business and I added that I couldn't quit working for Kevin. After he heard me out, he looked at me with considerable disappointment. He was conflicted and unable to adopt a firm stance. It wasn't until the next day that he shared his thoughts. He decided that I was selling my services thanks to the connections I obtained through the bank and that I was doing it during work hours, so I should share my profits with the bank. He figured that I wouldn't agree to the bank's claim on my profits, so he gave me an ultimatum: either I resign from the bank and run my business, or I change the terms of my employment. The terms of my new contract entailed a promotion to a managerial position, which also came with a raise. However, in order to get that promotion, I would have to land an investment project for the bank by myself within the first month. In addition, from now on, it would be my responsibility to sell the bank's services.

   I didn't have to think it over because I still didn't want to leave the bank. I accepted the chance for a promotion and I resolutely told Frank that I would find a new project for the bank. It was only after I left the office that I realized what I was up against. When I talked about throwing myself in at the deep end before, I meant walking out of my room where porno was playing on my laptop in order to take up work in auditing. Now I was about to dive into some really deep water. I was still in my twenties, and businesspeople often treated me like a child on the playground. Even though I had already committed to selling Kevin's services, the investment bank dealt with transactions that were often worth several hundred times more. However, I switched off this negative thinking. I remembered the path that had led me here, what skills I had acquired, how strong my self-control was, and how solid the attitude I had built was. I couldn't give up now and go back to being a fearful young man in front of a computer screen watching pornography.

   I wanted to move up to the next level, so I started to act. I started with gaining experience in sales by setting up several meetings regarding Kevin's services. They all went just like the one with Mr. Anders, with one exception. A potential client asked me, "What are you doing here, little boy?" Of course, I wanted to talk back, but I bit my tongue. I thanked him for his time and invited him to contact me if he ever changed his mind about me. You might expect that this situation threw me off my game, but I was pleased with my self-control and I gained even more power to prove that I am no longer a little boy. I returned to the office and began to work hard on finding a project for my bank. Then it occurred to me that Kevin, before I joined his company, had provided a lot of services for entrepreneurs who were not clients of my bank. I met with him almost immediately. I notified him about the very good contract I'd signed with Mr. Anders and about the meetings with other businesspeople. He was happy to hear this news. Then I asked him to tell me about the projects they had carried out so far: who he was doing them for, how they were progressing, and most importantly, whether he had heard of any clients who were considering selling a business, taking over another company, or securing financing. Kevin told me about his various clients for a long time, but only one had confided in him the details of his business. It turned out that one of the breweries for which Kevin had provided services was thinking about rapidly expanding his business in the face of high demand for their products. In a flash, I contacted the owner of the brewery and arranged a meeting.

The owner of the brewery confirmed that he was indeed looking for financing for his company. He keenly listened to my offer, but said that we weren't the first investment bank to approach him. Then, I calmly told him about our experience, presented our bank managers, and stressed that investment funds had praised our professionalism. I thought that the owner would consider my offer and possibly get back to me, but to my surprise he replied that he remembered Kevin fondly—his service for the brewery earned them a decent profit—so he would trust me as well. It worked out: I brought the bank a contract for consultancy on financing the expansion of the brewery. I didn't lose my job, but I was promoted and I continued working with Kevin. Now, free to do business, I was the face of both the bank's services and Kevin's, and not just among the business contacts that I had made so far.

This story ends here because this part happened quite recently. In the meantime, I have undertaken several other ventures, but it is too early to write about them. Another project that I have completed was writing this book. For over a year, in my spare time, I wrote down my story and poured onto paper the knowledge which has helped me so much. The situations I described leave no doubt that the ability to interact with people has not only helped me, but it has enabled me to do business. Social intelligence turned out to be crucial for me. Thanks to walking away from pornography, I became more empathic; I began to show people more understanding and to feel the joy of spending time with them. The relationships I built this way helped me to develop a functioning business. In the end, I became valuable to many people, including those unconnected with business. Interestingly, I abandoned my previous attitude of a greedy fast talker, which also had an impact on my image. The very fact that I had become patient and thoughtful caused people to look at me differently.

It paid to look for good opportunities and to calmly wait for them, because better or worse opportunities appear all the time. The whole path that I travelled from my first efforts to abandon pornography to my successes in business was full of ups and downs. However, at some point I realized that instead of making pointless attempts, it is better to earnestly work on my self-improvement and to give myself a chance to find truly good opportunities. By bettering myself, I almost completely got rid of my weaknesses and reinforced my strengths, which has prepared me for serious endeavors. I agree that it's always worth trying in business, but sometimes it's better to devote time and energy to acquiring the necessary knowledge and experience. Of course, it does happen that people immediately find a good business on their first try. Remember, however, that everything requires a lot of determination and self-control, which won't be easy to achieve without balance in your body.

It's hard for me to believe how big a transformation I have undergone in just a few years. From a reckless little brat who delighted in laziness, losing lots of time and energy to pornography, I gradually turned into a mature man who you can count on. Many readers may say that I owe my achievements to my self-development and good decisions, but the truth is that what led me here was quitting pornography. If it hadn't been for this step, I wouldn't have been able to get to know my real self, to see my own potential; I wouldn't have gained the experience, patience, or self-control.

When I was writing this book, I came across a lot of people who, like me, noticed the beneficial effect of discontinuing pornography. Not everyone has gotten rich, but most of them were working on their happiness in life. Many of these people have started to seriously pursue their professional and family lives, while others have pursued their passions. We all agree, however, that a few-months-long effort to break out of the clutches of our habit has been rewarded bountifully.

The fact that some people find it so difficult to part with pornography tends to raise the eyebrows of others. This is because the quality and availability of today's pornography is very highly addictive, and the almost unlimited potential for novelty make it impossible to get bored with it. In addition, there is a whole hormonal mechanism and reward system that misinterprets this artificial stimuli, suggesting that the body desperately needs them. Breaking out of this addiction is a tall order for a weak body and a weak mind—but for a strong body and a strong mind, this doesn't pose a major problem. Now that my body is strong and running smoothly, and my mind is well-aware of the mechanisms associated with pornography and masturbation, it is very easy for me to abstain from these stimuli. It doesn't change the fact that I remember how I behaved before and how tough it was for me to quit. The inclination toward unnatural erotic stimuli was a great lesson for me, and abandoning them strengthened me later in life. Thanks to this, I learned patience and self-control, which are valuable qualities in adult life. Life is too beautiful to squander on illusory pleasures and to give up what it has to offer. It is much easier to learn this truth by keeping the body and mind in a state of balance.

10. EXPERIENCE OF SOCIETY

To rectify past blunders is impossible, but we might profit by the experience of them.

- George Washington

10.1. OLDER TEACHINGS

The whole world of mankind—now and in the past—has faced the same problem. If pornography and masturbation weren't taboo, we would have thousands of studies and conclusions about how to deal with them. Unfortunately, these issues are embarrassing and opinions on them have been more and more divided recently. For centuries, conservative society had condemned masturbation and the display of the naked body: for a long time it could only be seen in paintings and sculptures. It wasn't until the twentieth century that people first voiced the opinion that masturbation is not harmful, and that it even has health benefits. The most common argument in support of these claims is that ejaculation cleanses the reproductive organs and helps get rid of any cancer cells that may have potentially formed there. Others argue that arousal and regular stimulation of the reproductive system increases one's sex drive. It's difficult to refute these theories—if we consider sporadic masturbation, without the aid of pornography. However, people who formulate such statements do not take into account the abuse of the reproductive system which results from using the high-quality pornography which is currently available.

Unfortunately, people—especially young people—who come across lenient opinions on masturbation may come to the conclusion that frequent masturbation and watching pornography are harmless. They couldn't be more wrong. All of the chapters of this book deal with the harmful effects of abusing these stimuli. The consequences of masturbating too frequently contradict the theses about the positive aspects of masturbation. It leads to a number of unpleasant problems associated with the male reproductive system, adversely affects one's attitude in life, and brings a number of other lamentable effects, which I have already discussed in more detail in the previous chapters. So, have people been condemning masturbation for centuries because it's potentially unhealthy? Or perhaps they noticed the problems it causes? It's worth taking a closer look at the most popular moral teachings from around the world. If we can explore the science of humanity, it is better to do it than to learn about the consequences of this risky behavior on one's own.

Most cultures of the modern world originate from the major religions that have passed on their beliefs to generations for hundreds—and sometimes thousands—of years.[89] Religions are usually characterized by stringent restrictions or requirements, but they are also an abundant source of knowledge. Moreover, religions served as a way to organize societies. For thousands of years, they have developed rules that were meant to ensure the common good and the long, prosperous lives of individuals. Most of them are based on similar assumptions, for example, ones as obvious as "do not kill or steal." Most are also critical of a dissolute lifestyle. The prohibition of sex before marriage ("do not commit adultery") may have been aimed at curbing the transmission of venereal diseases. It is possible that it was also intended to prevent chaotic reproduction, resulting, for example, in the breeding of closely related people. Many of the world's religions also condemned masturbation before there was easily accessible, high-quality pornography. It is worth noting that many mathematical, biological, or astrological discoveries were the work of monks who conducted meticulous research while exercising abstinence. It's funny to think that if religions hadn't prescribed celibacy and hadn't condemned masturbation, monks and other scientists—instead of counting integrals and teaching successive generations—would have masturbated for days on end. And today, instead of using the Internet, we would still be using homing pigeons.

It wasn't Christians who began to spread sexual abstinence and freedom from the bondage of impure thoughts. In the oldest known times, masturbation was frowned upon, but most often this stemmed from a lack of

---

[89] I am not a theologian or a religious scholar, and the following information comes from the research of online resources. I have also sometimes included the opinions of forum users.

knowledge about the human reproductive system and the human body in general. Hippocrates (5th century BC) believed that semen is derived from and stored in the whole body, especially in the head. Interestingly, perhaps rightly, he noted that sexual abstinence positively affects a male's physiology and emotional state, preventing depression, for example. In antiquity, semen was perceived as a liquid that animated the body. It was concluded that its loss causes various disorders, and that excessive use of sexual pleasures leads to many ailments. Inflammatory diseases of the reproductive system and gonorrhea were attributed to the consequences of sperm loss. Hippocrates terms diseases originating from lasciviousness (including from masturbation) "tabes dorsalis," which translates as "wasting of the back." Epicurus claimed that the seed is an element of the soul and of the body. Other scientists thought that semen proceeds from and travels down the spinal cord.

In ancient Rome, care was taken to prevent the vice of masturbation and to preserve purity using special instruments. One of the most prominent Roman physicians, Caelius Aurelianus (5th century AD), recommended the application of a lead plate to one's testicles, so as not to stimulate the genitals. Galen (2nd century AD) had a different opinion, claiming that draining semen from the body is healthy and necessary. He claimed that semen retained in the body decomposes and poison a man.

In the Middle Ages, the moral ideal was temperance, so sexual activities, including masturbation, were condemned and considered sinful. In the eighteenth century, Samuel-Auguste Tissot—a doctor from Lausanne, Switzerland—published a work entitled *Onanism: a Dissertation on the Diseases Caused by Masturbation*, in which he attributed many maladies to masturbation, including infertility, epilepsy, rheumatism, blindness, gonorrhea, hemorrhoids, madness, mental retardation, premature death, and suicide. In the nineteenth century, psychiatrists recognized masturbation as the cause of many mental illnesses, while

Jean-Étienne Dominique Esquirol regarded it as the result of such illnesses. It wasn't until the twentieth century that the development of sexology allowed the majority of these false views on sexuality, reproductive organs, and masturbation to be overthrown.

Judaic culture commands people to reproduce. This fact led to the strict commandment that a sexual act must lead to the transfer of semen to the vagina. Thousands of years ago, these precepts had also defined the frequency of sexual intercourse to which a spouse would be entitled, depending on what profession he had: once every 6 months for a sailor, once a month for a man riding a camel, once a week for a man riding on a donkey, twice a week for a laborer, and every day for a financially stable man.[90] One possible inference from these recommendations is that only after achieving financial stability can one afford sex and ejaculation on a daily basis. Perhaps Judaism also predicted that excessive sexual activity causes a loss of zeal for work and a loss of motivation. Generally, in this religion, any form of sexual contact within a marriage is permitted, unless it is associated with ejaculation outside the vagina. Orthodox Judaism definitively outlaws masturbation for men, but it is a rabbinical prohibition, not a Torah-based one.

The ban is so strict that the following entry appears in the Talmud: "In the case of a man, the hand that reaches below the navel should be chopped off" (Niddah 13a).[91] The basis for this tenet of Judaism and Christianity is the story in the Book of Genesis in which Judah instructs his son Onan to have offspring with his late brother's widow. "Onan knew that the seed should not be his; ...when he

---

[90] Paul Jedwab "My Jewish Learning": *Traditional Sources on Sexual Pleasure: Some classical Jewish statements about sex might surprise you.*

[91] "Judaism 101": *Kosher Sex*; http://www.jewfaq.org/sex.htm

went in unto his brother's wife, he spilled his seed on the ground, lest that he should give seed to his brother. And the thing that he did displeased the Lord: wherefore he slew him."[92] God's condemnation of Onan was seen as proof that masturbation, and specifically the waste of semen, is unacceptable. And so the name "onanism" was coined from Onan's name. The reasoning behind the ban on masturbation is that the function of sexuality is to strengthen the relationship between a woman and a man, in addition to procreation. Masturbation is the destruction of the semen, the source of life, in a way that neither engenders human existence, nor deepens one's relationship with a woman. In addition, controlling one's sexual impulses distinguishes humans from animals, and masturbation is a manifestation of a lack of self-discipline. Conservative Judaism and reformed Judaism regard the act of masturbation not as a sin, because Onan's misdeed is not identified as masturbation, but as contesting his father's will.

According to stereotypes, the group of people who most easily accumulates wealth are Jews. People often mistakenly deduce that among the reclusive Jewish society there are secret instructions on how to get rich. In truth, however, the road to wealth may go hand in hand with the traditional rules, customs, and humble living of Jews, which includes the area of sex life.

Buddhism urges lay people to refrain from improper sexual behavior and asks novices (those who want to become monks) and secular people who are pious in their religious practice to abstain from any sexual activity.[93] The Buddha said that it is good to follow these recommendations, but that they must not be imposed on anyone. The essence of Buddhism is to leave the Samsara

---

[92] Genesis 38, 9–10.

[93] Wikipedia: *Religious views on masturbation*

cycle, that is, the cycle of rebirth in various forms depending on the state of our karma. What helps us to achieve this goal is—for instance—meditating and following the Noble Eightfold Path, which the above-mentioned tenets are part of. Mastering sexual passion, which is one of the causes of suffering and rebirth, is supposed to facilitate one's journey on this path. For someone who wants to achieve liberation, masturbation constitutes an obstacle. Nevertheless, Buddhism admits that masturbation is a natural manifestation of sexual drive as long as it doesn't overly absorb us and doesn't replace normal sexual relations between a woman and a man.

Buddha encouraged his students to be abstinent and even to live in celibacy. Monks not only decide to live in celibacy, but also pledge to overcome their desires. According to the Sūtra of the Upāsaka Precepts, masturbation is inappropriate sexual behavior. In any country where Buddhism is a major religion (China, South Korea, Laos, Vietnam, or Thailand), pornography is forbidden. Some Taoists argue that masturbation lowers energy levels in men. This is because ejaculation through masturbation limits one's vital life energy: qi. According to them, sex with a woman differs from masturbation in that the partners supplement each other's qi. The Taoists believe that martial arts should not be practiced earlier than 48 hours after masturbation (others extend this time up to 6 months) because it takes so long to regenerate the qi lost during masturbation. Semen is an extremely precious substance. Some people think that a bowl of food is worth as much as a drop of blood, and a glass of blood as much as a drop of semen.

Hindu scriptures also describe masturbation as a sin. Masturbation is forbidden mainly for unmarried men. In the *Brihadaranyaka Upanishad,* it is written that bone marrow, cerebral fluid, and sperm are composed of synthetic blood components.[94] They should not be wasted in masturbation, which is aided by fantasy. One of the texts refers specifically to masturbation and provides atonement for this sin. If the host willingly unloads his seed by any means other than intercourse with a woman, he should chant a verse from the Gayathri mantra a thousand times and should perform a breathing exercise (Pranayama) three times.[95] In the case of apprentices, the sin is heavier because it involves breaking their vows.

In religions with Christian roots, masturbation is a sin. It is considered an immature experience of sexuality, a misuse of sexuality which goes against its purpose. It causes estrangement from the bond of marriage and from fertility. Its consequences include an excessive focus on physicality, which leads to addiction. Masturbation is also responsible for the following:
- it hampers the motivation for developing oneself and obstructs the search for joy in other areas of life;
- it pushes people to clam up and isolate themselves from society;
- it encourages loneliness;
- it causes a build-up of physical tension, which becomes increasingly difficult to satisfy; and
- it is the cause of psychological tension and guilt.

Catholicism emphasizes that humans are not always equally responsible for their sins. There are various justifications for wrongful acts, such as immaturity or being misled. Therefore, if someone was told that masturbation is good, then he needn't feel guilty for it.

In Islam, masturbation is *haram*, meaning forbidden.[96]

---

[94] Wikipedia: *Brihadaranyaka Upanishad*

[95] http://hinduism.stackexchange.com/questions/697/what-does-hinduism-say-about-masturbation/704

[96] Wikipedia: *Islam and masturbation*

Sunnis generally do not accept masturbation, apart from extenuating circumstances. They encourage Muslims to fast in order to control the sexual desire arising from not finding someone to marry. In situations of overwhelming tension, masturbation is permissible and treated like eating pork when you are hungry and other foods are unavailable. Masturbation during the day invalidates fasting and requires ablution—a thorough, ritual washing of the body. During Ramadan, Muslims may not masturbate. According to Shiites, any sexual activity outside of marriage is a sin. The Quran stipulates that believers must protect their reproductive organs and can only show them to their spouse (this is unacceptable in any other situation). Anyone who seeks a different way to satisfy their lust is a criminal.

Most religions, despite their different roots, have a similar, negative attitude towards masturbation. Is it possible that so many people in the world are wrong? Is it possible that over a billion believers feel guilty after masturbation, while pop culture thinks it is pleasant and good for them? In our times, we are skeptical in our approach to theses put forward by religion. It's rare for religions to concretely and logically explain their prohibitions. This is probably because theologians and thinkers did not have access to advanced medicine, science, and the various tools available nowadays. However, there is very strong argumentation to support their reasoning. The theses were anchored in vast experience and hundreds of years of observing people. It was probably noticed that masturbation is destructive to society. The men who engaged in masturbation ceased to be productive and did not start families. They stayed on the sidelines of their local communities. They became secretive, selfish, and overly focused on physicality. It was also observed that sexual stimuli are not conducive to self-mastery, to which almost all religions attach great importance. In most religions, the regularity of rituals, prayers, and meditations plays a significant role. They foster self-control and help maintain a peace of mind.

10.2. SPORT

Another area for which masturbation and sex are sticking points is sports. All athletes want to know if sexual activity beforehand helps or hinders their chances. In men, the level of testosterone during competition is important, and the explanation comes down to this. As I mentioned in the previous chapters, sex with a partner can be a cause for a substantial increase in testosterone, while masturbation does not cause considerable changes in testosterone levels in the short-term, it can lower it in the long run. Additionally, there are a number of arguments for or against sexual activity: it reduces aggression; it helps concentration by decreasing tension; by increasing testosterone levels, it increases efficiency; it flushes out internal energy; it tires the body. These arguments, however, don't hold water or are inconsistent with reality, because, for example, physical exercise during sex is not a big deal for professional athletes.

In accordance with what I recounted in the previous chapters, there is no doubt about the bad influence of masturbation on anything a man does, and when it comes to sex with a partner, it probably has both advantages and disadvantages. For now, it has been proven that sexual activity a short time (up to 2 hours) before doing sports is detrimental.[97] What definitely disqualifies sexual activity from important events is that it can disrupt our motivation. One of the main drivers of a man's actions is reproduction and until we reproduce, we still feel an internal strength that rallies us to do our best. After sexual gratification, we lose one of the strongest motivating forces for a human

---

[97] Laura Stefani, Giorgio Galanti, Johnny Padulo, Nicola L. Bragazzi, Nicola Maffulli (2016): *Sexual Activity before Sports Competition: A Systematic Review.*

being. What's more, after sexual activity we become less sensitive to dopamine, and as we already know, motivation is essentially a small dose of dopamine. If the system gets abused with high doses of dopamine during masturbation or sex, we may not feel the motivation pushing us toward victory.

In martial arts, motivation and rivalry play key roles. Nearly 100% of boxing trainers categorically forbid their boxers from engaging in sexual activity before the fight. Few people talk publicly about their sex life, but several well-known athletes, such as Muhammad Ali and Manny Pacquiao, have openly admitted to exercising abstinence a few weeks before the fight. Of course, there will be those for whom sexual activity before an important performance encourages better results, so you should find out for yourself which approach is better.

10.3. THE PORNOGRAPHY INDUSTRY

The sex industry definitely has the biggest influence on customs related to sexuality. This industry promotes the viewing of pornography and masturbation as normal activities. Is watching strangers copulating normal? Of course not. Before there were movies or pornographic magazines, the equivalent of modern pornography was peeping at people. Can you imagine someone climbing up a wall to a bedroom window at night so as to peer furtively at others' sexual escapades? Such delinquents quickly ended up behind bars and were always stigmatized as perverts. Admittedly, an important detail in this case is the invasion of privacy without their victims' consent. However, the fact that they had a tendency to peep at people branded them as perverts. Currently, the industry makes it possible to share your intimacy in exchange for money, but is it normal to enter someone's intimate zone without getting to know them, gaining their trust, and reciprocating a minimum of feelings? No. Pornography is easily available, but watching it is a type of perversion. What's worse is that frequent viewing of pornography and the gradually weaker reactions of the reward system to the familiar types of porn make us look for new, exciting varieties, which leads to more and more perversions and new fetishes.

Unfortunately, the pursuit of another influx of dopamine often results in scouring the darkest corners of the Internet. This is supported by the intelligent algorithms of pornography websites that are able to offer us almost infinite doses of novelty. At first, men naturally shy away from excessive fetishes, but over time they succumb to gentle suggestions on the website or they unwittingly play films which show new, unexpected scenes and situations, such as group sex, for example. Such a mechanism slowly lulls their defenses to sleep. After some time, porn enthusiasts no longer feel inhibited and check out other categories of adult content.

Frequent masturbation and watching pornography can cause a drop in testosterone levels, and it sometimes happens that a man begins to doubt his sexuality. Low testosterone and reaching for pornography involving, say, transgender and homosexual people often leads to suspicions that one is also homosexual. I won't go deeper into the topic, or describe what this can do to you. In forums for men recovering from addiction to pornography and masturbation, the victims describe how they hit rock bottom after being guided by the casual recommendations of algorithms on pornography websites. Unfortunately, each bottom is covered by layers of sludge which can permanently damage one's psyche, which I hope none of you discover personally. The worst thing is that this mechanism can turn normal people into fetishists and perverts, who later have a hard time returning to normalcy. The publishers of pornography websites want to make you as attached to their website as possible, so they strive to interest you in the largest imaginable number of fetishes that are hard to find in normal life.

Another issue is that the viewers quickly get bored with individual porn actresses. This is due to the constant search for novelty. The performers know this very well because they are familiar with precise statistics about the viewership of their movies and they do everything they can to retain viewers for as long as possible. It is common practice to interact with the audience, by meeting fans or publishing an email address. Fans send messages to their favorite actresses where they write about their feelings and express their gratitude for the pleasure the actresses give them. The office also sends a nice response on their behalf encouraging them to continue visiting the actress' website, to pay for a subscription, maintain relations, or get them to become infatuated.

Equally puzzling is the participation of actors in this industry. Mostly, they begin their careers in acting or modeling. With the temptation of easy money, they are drawn step by step into bolder productions. It is only when they realize what they are actually doing that the problem begins. The industry reduces sexuality to mechanical movements, and the actors are treated like bags of meat. There is no place for humanity or feelings in movies. A porn actor's career usually ends very soon and often accompanied by a nervous breakdown. There are a lot of interviews with former porn actors on the Internet who talk about their experiences and the reasons for which they decided to part ways with the industry. Very often, it is also an embarrassing chapter in a biography which the actors prefer not to admit to. Of course, there are also actors who work in the industry for a long time and who years after retiring still remember their career fondly. Many of them start producing films on their own. In the end, it is still a lucrative business, but with very high costs to society.

The salaries of the actors are less than staggering: from several hundred to several thousand dollars per performance.[98] However, the entire industry is worth around $100 billion[99] (about 10% of which comes from the US), produces several thousand movies each year, and generates about $15 billion in profits. The global production of pornography is so effective that it already accounts for over 10% of the total Internet. In 2016 alone, one of the most popular pornographic sites displayed about 4.6 billion hours of movies, or about 524,000 years' worth, while YouTube's watch time amounted to about 46,000 years. The most popular pornography websites obtain revenues from advertisements and paid subscriptions, and their value exceeds several billion dollars. Considering the type of content and the numerous obstacles created by governments to protect their citizens, the industry is doing quite well and is still gaining new viewers. At the moment, there are many organizations trying to counteract the spread of pornography,[100] but given the great temptation that pornographic content becomes, it is still a difficult struggle. The greatest strength in this uphill battle is our ability to ignore pornography and the education of our loved ones for their own well-being.

---

[98] Chris Morris "CNBC" (2016): *Porn's dirtiest secret: What everyone gets paid.*

[99] "CNBC" (2015): *Things Are Looking Up in America's Porn Industry.*

[100] See, for example, http://fightthenewdrug.org ; http://rewardfoundation.org

11. DO YOUR BEST

The only man who never makes a mistake is the man who never does anything.

- Theodore Roosvelt

Everyone makes mistakes. It's important not to beat yourself up over the past for too long. Just be sure not to repeat the same mistakes in the future. When I realized that the world offers almost unlimited possibilities, and in my heyday I was watching strangers fornicate online, I was in very bad shape. My addiction had lasted about 7 years, and

I considered them lost years. Almost every evening before falling asleep, until late at night, I imagined how I might have used my time differently if I had never seen a pornographic movie. How I would have spent my energy and where I would be then. I resented myself, but even more so I resented my friends and family, who allowed such strong stimuli to reach such a young mind.

When I used to watch pornography, I was lazy and unruly. I couldn't see the beauty of the world around me. Nothing seemed to have any purpose to me. I squandered a lot of time and energy, and fear prevented me from using my remaining resources. In the end, only my own fleeting pleasure was important. It is sad that this happened, and when I managed to break this habit I was overwhelmed by an equally destructive bitterness. Only after some time did I realize that I would never have this time back and that I had to go on living, whatever tomorrow may bring. We must treat every mistake like a lesson, and after each fall, we must get up and move on. I received a powerful lesson because turning to pornography and masturbation was a huge mistake. However, it's a waste of time to dwell on the past; it's much better to devote this energy to the future.

My victory over my addiction required a lot of strength. The struggle with temptation, my weakness, and the tension was one of the most demanding battles I have ever fought. I triumphed and as a reward I gained the power to act. The self-control which I gained allowed me to develop myself, to get an education, to take care of my health, and to handle stress in difficult situations—and above all, it taught me to persevere in the pursuit of my goals. On the road to success, the most important thing is to be tenacious and immune to adversity. It should also be remembered that a lot of stimuli are lying in wait to divert our attention away from those goals. Since then, I have been skeptical about all the incentives around me. Even though I have overcome such a strong stimulus as pornography, I still have to be careful not to get involved in social media, to avoid the surplus of unnecessary information, and not to overdo it with other seemingly useful activities. I always deliberate over whether new knowledge is indeed something I will really need.

Remember, a lot of businesses are constantly vying for our attention. Even when it comes to a healthy lifestyle, they strive for the maximum possible attention from us. For example, it is in the interest of many manufacturers that consumers develop insecurities about their appearance and spend hundreds of dollars on cosmetics, supplements, or personal training. Unfortunately, getting engrossed in improving our appearance can steal valuable time and draw us away from more important goals. Another example is personal development specialists who aim to make us addicted to their beautiful words and maniacally buy their books or training sessions. You should be alert and keep in mind that often under the guise of help there lies a profitable business. Therefore, we must always adopt a path of moderation, remember what is most important to us and, above all, always control ourselves. If we want to succeed and fulfill our dreams and the dreams of our loved ones, we must cultivate self-control in every aspect of life and make sure that unnecessary stimuli don't distract our attention. Self-control will help us become better, stronger, and more effective in our activities.

Keep in mind that combating your weaknesses cannot be your only goal. It was thanks to the fact that I wanted to lead a happy life, to find my better half, to travel, and to not worry about money that I was able to overcome my weaknesses. It was a coincidence that, wishing to practice self-control, I weaned myself off of pornography. On the other hand, if I hadn't spent time watching porn for 7 years, maybe I wouldn't have needed to exercise my self-control. Easy access to a source of high dopamine doses impaired my development and my ability to cope in less-comfortable situations. So I had to break this habit. Quitting pornography and masturbation without a higher goal in mind can be much more challenging.

If you want to quit pornography and feel the benefits of this change, do it once and for all. Only after a few months will your reward system and endocrine system return to a balance. A gradual abandonment of pornography, for example, limiting sessions to one movie, returning less frequently, or looking for alternatives will not work. That will only cause even more frustration than before. If you want to experience the benefits resulting from the discontinuation of pornography, you must do it definitively, forever. It will be helpful to avoid all sexual stimuli and situations in which your self-control is vulnerable, and to have a strategy of what to do when there are urges. Another thing that can thwart these attempts is to exaggerate its power. It may be difficult to overcome the addiction, but if we don't think about it and steer clear of stimuli and situations we associate with this habit, then things are going to go much more smoothly for us. We must not trivialize pornography and masturbation. Despite its popularity, it is still a serious stimulant and is very harmful to one's body, mind, and behavior. A lot of people may spend time on pornography, but it is still a perversion. We should keep in mind that voyeurism of strangers performing sexual acts is not normal. No matter how popular it is, it is still behavior that jars with human nature.

The main reason why I completely stopped watching pornography and started to avoid all other sexual stimuli was my desire to get rich and have a happy life. Building wealth required my mind to be sharp in order to help me count and deduce efficiently. My mind had to be creative so that I could find ways to make money. When I quit pornography, all these features began to sharpen and actually contributed to my success. The reward system began to easily sense the smallest doses of dopamine responsible for motivation and improved efficiency. I started to learn more capably and to apply the knowledge in practice. Better ideas—and more of them—began to come to me, and the search for ideas itself and inventing new products began to bring me great joy.

Building wealth also required that I learn how to interact with people. I had to learn how to be more empathetic, how to talk and persuade, and above all how to be a valuable person for others. These features also improved considerably thanks to my discontinuation of porn. My balanced hormonal system helped me feel at ease with people and to remember my worth, and my reward system allowed me to derive happiness from spending time with others.

Building wealth also required courage and perseverance in problematic situations. Thanks to quitting pornography, I began to live my life and to deal with many difficult problems, which was character-building. A balanced body provided me with testosterone—so valuable when taking risks. I began to feel confident at the negotiating table and while investing money. Thanks to my discontinuation of pornography, I was able to keep my cool and not panic when situations got out of control. I also became responsible and accepted every loss with understanding.

Getting rich also required patience from me. Giving up pornography helped me avoid making hasty decisions and taking premature actions. I learned to patiently wait for the rewards and fruits of my labor. Thanks to my patience, I saw the positive effects of quitting pornography and masturbation. All of these qualities have made me a better man. And I owe it all to the decision to abandon pornography and masturbation first of all, but also to the few months during which I abstained from all sexual stimuli, and finally to the balance of my body which eventually returned. These things gave me exceptional strength to pursue success.

I won't rest on my laurels, though. I'm constantly working on myself and trying to be a better version of myself every day. There are still many things to do, ideas to discover, and places to visit. I have started to get rich: I have a good job and a prospering business, but I still haven't set up a real company that would offer products on a large scale and give employment to many people in need. I still haven't hit on a big idea and I haven't discovered innovations that will help improve the world and be a real contribution to society. I still don't have a yacht to sail around the world on. I don't do enough public service. I still see a lot of injustice in the world which needs to be resolved in order to bring people relief. None of these problems will be answered if we waste time on the illusory pleasure of pornography and masturbation. The world will not advance if we allow for procrastination and the waste of people's potential.

Remember, life is more than just a temporary injection of dopamine and a release of tension. It is a pity to waste life on this deceptive pleasure. If you have a problem with walking away from pornography and masturbation, then the knowledge presented here will certainly make it much easier for you. Abandoning the use of porn can strengthen you on many other levels in life and can help you achieve your dreams. As my example shows, steering clear of all this can bring a number of benefits. I have long been convinced of all the mechanisms associated with this problem and it is only after many years that I can be sure that avoiding unnecessary sexual stimuli is the right path to take. Thanks to this book, you can dispel your doubts much faster. If you have a problem with pornography, solve it and start living anew, using your potential freely. Be strong and expect much more from life than a picture or a movie with a naked, attractive woman. In the end, I'd like to thank you for spending your time reading my book. I have made every effort to ensure that what I have written is helpful to you and that the knowledge I have provided is valuable. If you find this material worthwhile, please recommend it to others in need. I wish you good luck and I hope you find joy in your life.

AFTERWORD

We don't just hope to get rich, but we are already doing so. Passing luxury cars on the street or browsing technological innovations, we no longer dream about possessing them, but we wonder whether these items will be useful to us, and we calculate the means needed for their purchase. Travel has not only become achievable, but is an everyday occurrence, a normal part of our lives. We develop business globally, visit clients all over the world, and earn money from anywhere on Earth with Internet access. In our free time, we pursue our passions, surf some waves, or help the needy. We don't dream about tabloid models because we have our beloved soulmates, which are the only ones, the most beautiful women in the world for us. Our past dreams have become commonplace events or realistic plans that we implement with enthusiasm and satisfaction every day. It gives us a lot more joy than watching a pornographic movie on a computer. Most importantly, this joy continues because we love life, what we do, and who we are.

RESOURCES

1. Pizzol D, Bertoldo A, Foresta C (2016): *Adolescents and web porn: a new era of sexuality.*
2. Brian Y. Park, Gary Wilson, Jonathan Berger, Matthew Christman, Bryn Reina, Frank Bishop, Warren P. Klam and Andrew P. Doan (2016): *Is Internet Pornography Causing Sexual Dysfunctions? A Review with Clinical Reports.*
3. Simone Kühn, Jürgen Gallinat (2014): *Brain Structure and Functional Connectivity Associated With Pornography Consumption: The Brain on Porn.*
4. Bronner G, Ben-Zion IZ (2014): *Unusual masturbatory practice as an etiological factor in the diagnosis and treatment of sexual dysfunction in young men.*
5. Paula Banca, Laurel S. Morris, Simon Mitchell, Neil A. Harrison, Marc N. Potenza, Valerie Voon (2015): *Novelty, conditioning and attentional bias to sexual rewards.*
6. Koukounas E, Over R (2000): *Changes in the magnitude of the eyeblink startle response during habituation of sexual arousal.*
7. National Institute on Drug Abuse (2016): *How does cocaine produce its effects?*
8. Gilbert SF (2000): *Developmental Biology. 6th edition.*
9. Exton NG, Truong TC, Exton MS, Wingenfeld SA, Leygraf N, Saller B, Hartmann U, Schedlowski M. (2000): *Neuroendocrine response to film-induced sexual arousal in men and women.*
10. Exton MS, Krüger TH, Bursch N, Haake P, Knapp

W, Schedlowski M, Hartmann U (2001): *Endocrine response to masturbation-induced orgasm in healthy men following a 3-week sexual abstinence*;
11. Scott I Zeitlin, MD and Jacob Rajfer, MD (2000): *Hyperprolactinemia and Erectile Dysfunction.*
12. Brody S, Krüger TH (2006): *The post-orgasmic prolactin increase following intercourse is greater than following masturbation and suggests greater satiety.*
13. John M. Grohol, Psy.D. (2006): *Orgasms Best in Sex vs. Masturbation.*
14. Romano-Torres M, Phillips-Farfán BV, Chavira R, Rodríguez-Manzo G, Fernández-Guasti A. (2007): *Relationship between sexual satiety and brain androgen receptors.*
15. Michelle J. Escasa, Jacqueline F. Casey, Peter B. Gray (2011): *Salivary Testosterone Levels in Men at a U.S. Sex Club.*
16. Dabbs JM Jr, Mohammed S (1992): *Male and female salivary testosterone concentrations before and after sexual activity.*
17. Tylka, T. L. (2015): *No harm in looking, right? Men's pornography consumption, body image, and well-being.*
18. Christian Laier, Matthias Brand (2017): *Mood changes after watching pornography on the Internet are linked to tendencies towards Internet-pornography-viewing disorder.*
19. Boies SC, Cooper A, Osborne CS (2004): *Variations in internet-related problems and psychosocial functioning in online sexual activities: implications for social and sexual development of young adults.*
20. Weaver JB 3rd, Weaver SS, Mays D, Hopkins GL, Kannenberg W, McBride D (2010): *Mental- and physical-health indicators and sexually explicit media use behavior by adults.*
21. Valerie Voon, Thomas B. Mole, Paula Banca, Laura

Porter, Laurel Morris, Simon Mitchell, Tatyana R. Lapa, Judy Karr, Neil A. Harrison, Marc N. Potenza, Michael Irvine (2014): *Neural Correlates of Sexual Cue Reactivity in Individuals with and without Compulsive Sexual Behaviours.*
22. Andreas G. Philaretou, Ahmed Y. Mahfouz, Katherine R. Allen (2005): *Use of Internet Pornography and Men's Well-Being.*
23. Kasper TE, Short MB, Milam AC. (2014): *Narcissism and Internet pornography use.*
24. Walton MT, Cantor JM, Lykins AD (2015): *An Online Assessment of Personality, Psychological, and Sexuality Trait Variables Associated with Self-Reported Hypersexual Behavior.*
25. Stephanie S. Luster, Larry J. Nelson, Franklin O. Poulsen, Brian J. Willoughby (2013): *Emerging Adult Sexual Attitudes and Behaviors: Does Shyness Matter?*
26. Laier C, Schulte FP, Brand M (2012): *Pornographic picture processing interferes with working memory performance.*
27. Lester W. Wright Jr., Henry E. Adams (2010): *The effects of stimuli that vary in erotic content on cognitive processes.*
28. Steven B. Most, Stephen D. Smith, Amy B. Cooter, Bethany N. Levy, David H. Zald (2007): *The naked truth: Positive, arousing distractors impair rapid target perception.*
29. Laier C, Pawlikowski M, Brand M (2014): *Sexual picture processing interferes with decision-making under ambiguity.*
30. Beyens I., Vandenbosch L., Eggermont S. (2015): *Early adolescent boys' exposure to Internet pornography: Relationships to pubertal timing, sensation seeking, and academic performance.*
31. Dan Ariely George Loewenstein (2005): *The heat of the moment: the effect of sexual arousal on sexual*

decision making.
32. S.Kühn, J.Gallinat (2016): *Chapter Three - Neurobiological Basis of Hypersexuality.*
33. Baumeister RF, Bratslavsky E, Muraven M, Tice DM (1998): *Ego depletion: is the active self a limited resource?*
34. Malte Friese, Wilhelm Hofmann (2009): *Control me or I will control you: Impulses, trait self-control, and the guidance of behaviour.*
35. Klaus-Helmut Schmidt, Marlen Hupke, Stefan Diestel (2012): *Does dispositional capacity for self-control attenuate the relation between self-control demands at work and indicators of job strain?*
36. Roy F. Baumeister, Matthew Gailliot, C. Nathan DeWall, Megan Oaten (2006): *Self-Regulation and Personality: How Interventions Increase Regulatory Success, and How DepletionModerates the Effects of Traits on Behavior.*
37. Muraven M, Baumeister RF, Tice DM (1999): *Longitudinal improvement of self-regulation through practice: building self-control strength through repeated exercise.*
38. Oaten M, Cheng K. (2006): *Longitudinal gains in self-regulation from regular physical exercise.*
39. M. Oaten, K. Cheng (2007): *Improvements in self-control from financial monitoring.*"Journal of Economic Psychology".
40. Mark Muraven (2010): *Practicing Self-Control Lowers the Risk of Smoking Lapse.*
41. Lee N. Robins, Darlene H. Davis, David N. Nurco (1974): *How Permanent Was Vietnam Drug Addiction?*
42. Deborah C. Zetik, Alice F. Stuhlmacher (2002): *Goal Setting and Negotiation Performance: A Meta-Analysis.*
43. Andreas Jäger, David D. Loschelder, Malte Friese (2017): *Using Self-regulation to Successfully*

Overcome the Negotiation Disadvantage of Low Power.
44. Hengyi Rao, Marc Korczykowski, John Pluta, Angela Hoang, John A. Detre (2008): *Neural correlates of voluntary and involuntary risk taking in the human brain: An fMRI Study of the Balloon Analog Risk Task (BART).*
45. Coren L. Apicella, Anna Dreber, Benjamin Campbell, Peter B. Gray, Moshe Hoffman, Anthony C. Little (2008): *Testosterone and financial risk preferences.*
46. Thomas G. Travison, Andre B. Araujo, Amy B. O'Donnell, Varant Kupelian, John B. McKinlay (2007): *A Population-Level Decline in Serum Testosterone Levels in American Men.*
47. "Endocrine Society" (2012): *Declining testosterone levels in men not part of normal aging.*
48. J. M. Coates, J. Herbert (2008): *Endogenous steroids and financial risk taking on a London trading floor.*
49. Mattebo M, Tyden T, Häggström-Nordin E, Nillson KW (2014): *Pornography consumption, psychosomatic health and depressive symptoms among Swedish adolescents.*
50. Leppink EW, Chamberlain SR, Redden SA, Grant JE (2016): *Problematic sexual behavior in young adults: Associations across clinical, behavioral, and neurocognitive variables.*
51. Alec Sproten (2016): *How Abstinence Affects Preferences.*
52. Negash S, Sheppard NV, Lambert NM, Fincham FD (2016): *Trading Later Rewards for Current Pleasure: Pornography Consumption and Delay Discounting.*
53. Messina B, Fuentes D, Tavares H, Abdo CH, Scanavino MT (2017): *Executive Functioning of Sexually Compulsive and Non-Sexually Compulsive Men Before and After Watching an Erotic Video.*

54. Kacey Ballard, Brian Knutson (2009): *Dissociable neural representations of future reward magnitude and delay during temporal discounting.*
55. Laura Stefani, Giorgio Galanti, Johnny Padulo, Nicola L. Bragazzi, Nicola Maffulli (2016): *Sexual Activity before Sports Competition: A Systematic Review.*

Printed in France by Amazon
Brétigny-sur-Orge, FR